Published By Bull Dog Productions...

This being my first book writing and self-publishing experience, you may find a few flaws and mistakes in my lay out, grammah. ☺ And language use...But you have to remember...It's a dog narrating it ...Read with your heart Not your eyes...

Follow this beautiful Dog thru her life and after life adventures as her owners struggle with the loss of their best friend and companion. Jayden learns life on the streets can be lonely and scary, But finds love and compassion in the strangest of places... Narrated by a humorous, sassy Chow mix. When her life starts out, she is not too happy about being abused and kicked to the curbing, to the City's Dog Pen...Educated by her many new K9 friends, She charms a young couple to take a chance with her as head of security, And proves to be Mans (and woman's) BEST friend....After falling in Love with the neighbors handsome Labrador and living a pampered life. Her trip over the rainbow leaves her feeling guilty for inflicting heart ache and pain to her Mommy & Daddy. But with the help of new found friends, she repays the favor and mends their broken hearts even tho she can only be seen Thru a Dogs Eyes.

Hi...My name is Jayden....Yes ...THAT'S
RIGHT... I 'm a dog...Your probably saying to
yourself...Dogs can't talk...Never mind write a book...
Well if you're a dog lover...YOU know we can talk in
our own little ways. You just need to spend a little
time with us...Watch our faces, our body language,
our tails...Every little thing we do says something...
Well .... Ok... Not everything....Sometimes we just
have an itch that needs scratching... But we
communicate with our eyes...with the position of
our heads...The showing of our TEETH...ha ha
...Yah...You know what that one means.... We know
you humans communicate with one another... (We
just hear...Blah Blah Blah...) and you try to
communicate with us... (Once again Blah, Blah,
Blah...) You could read a book that tells you what a
dogs trying to say...But the only way to really know
how they feel......Is to give that dog a Home...Let him
or her into your heart.... Into your family...Into your
life...and keep them involved in your everyday
routines...Then...and only then...will you know how

it feels for them...Feel the love they have for you ...... the need they have for your love...Just as much as you will love them and need them.........Once they steal your Heart.

This book is dedicated to my humans...Jay & Kim Gafford... They rescued me..., cared for me..., and loved me.... When nobody else would...I hope you enjoy the story of my life. .as seen.... THRU A DOGS EYES...

Jayden Gafford

I started writing this book after Jayden had her first heart attack. That really got me thinking about her life and what she had been thru and what she was about to go thru...Writing it all down seemed to help ease the pain and heart ache I was having... She lived for an extra six months after that...and I am grateful for every day we had together...I passed up a trip to Italy so I could care for her during her last days....I couldn't handle it if she passed and I wasn't there for her.... She had been such a faithful pooch and a terrific watchdog...all around Man's BEST

Friend....She remained on this side of the rainbow until Kim returned from seeing family across the pond.....Soon after her return...Jayden had a bad seizure and Well ..I don't want to spoil the plot ...But I had the hardest decision of my Life to make and It came up fast....Loosing a family member is hard enough...But when you have to decide ...Has she been thru enough. Is she in Pain...What will her life be like if we try to extend it, any longer than we already have? Can she handle an operation ....the list goes on. Writing the first half was easy...It was her life....I thought I would have a hard time writing the rest...But as it turns out ...I was still writing about everyday life events ..I hope you enjoy Jayden's version of life and the afterlife thru my best friend's eyes... and... Please... Support your Local Animal shelters Thank you ... Jay & Kim Gafford

Hi ... My name is Jayden. You have just purchased a copy of Thru a Dogs Eyes. It is a story about my life. It may help when reading this book to use your best sassy voice... (Yeah. You know who I'm talking about ...YES! Her...Use HER voice.) I am not sassy all the time. It's just that...well ... Sometimes I get an attitude... cause...well.... because... uummm.... Well some of the time ......You humans are just plain stupid. Alright... There ... I said it. Well you're not stupid ALL the time. But, maybe you're just not paying attention. ALL right. Before you get all MAD! Let me just give you an example. If I chew on the car door. It's not because I like the taste of plastic and it's not that I'm hungry. Its cause you locked me in there with the windows all the way up. And I was really, really HOT! I didn't have any water, I was trying to get the door open or the window down and not having opposable thumbs makes it rather difficult. Do yah see where I am going with this? I know...I know ...That may have been a bit extreme. I was just trying to make a point and be funny......YES... it was at your expense...But THAT'S what makes it

funny.. Ha... Ha ha...Oops ... Sorry, Sorry, Maybe I
should just start over again...

Hi...My name is Jayden. I am a mixed breed Chow
Chow....I was born in East Providence Rhode Island.
Sometime in the fall of 1996. I don't know the exact
date because my very first pair of humans were...um
...to keep this rated PG...let's just say they were NOT
dog people. OK They didn't even know who my Daddy
was. He could have been a Golden retriever. As you
can see. I have got this silky golden fur mixed with the
faded browns and rust colors of the Chow Chow
breed...

Nobody knows for sure....I think my momma
was kinda easy, If you know what I'm saying, cause
come on, In today's day an age, join a dating service,
find yourself a nice pure breed stud on Craig's list or
something.... But anyway... I was born in East
Providence. I popped out with about 5 or 6 brother &
sisters. I don't even remember. It was so long ago... SO
here we are, about six of us, just drinking mother's

milk, peeing, pooping & sleeping. Nobody seemed too thrilled to have us around. Nobody picked us up or even cleaned up our messes. You can just imagine how ripe it was getting in that little wooden box. It smelled worse than low tide on a hot sunny day, if you catch my drift.

Then one day a pair of humans came in and took me away from all of that .They were kinda on the young side, a pretty girl and a young man. They seemed really nice, but what did I know. I could barely walk. Well they fell in love with me. Who could blame them? Dam! I was cute, almost too cute. HEY! DON'T laugh. You should have seen me, just a little ball of fluffy golden fur, with this fuzzy little tail that curled up over my back. I had a porky little body with wobbly little legs. I couldn't stand up for too long, never mind walk.

Well this couple loved me. I'd fall down and they would laugh and roll me over and rub my smooth white belly. Not being confined to that horrible little box, I was having quite the adventure at my new home. My new humans bought me tons of squeaky toys and gave me tasty treats all the time. Without all my brothers & sisters yelping and crawling all over me, I could sleep anytime, anywhere! In addition, not having to squat in my sibling poop and pee was a big step up. As for me, I could do my business anywhere I wanted too, every time in a clean fresh spot. No more sleeping in filth. Life was good! All except for this wacky little fur ball that scratched my nose. I just wanted to play. He hit me when I wasn't looking. Besides his bad attitude, I think he had a cat nip issue ... Now... I just stay far away from him...

So everything was going great. I had this big house all to myself. All the food I could eat, and clean place to sleep. Then one day my man human starts screaming and yelling. Something about stepping in crap all over the house and chewing his dress shoes. I don't even know what dress shoes are? Are they shoes that look like a dress or a dress that looks like a shoe? So the Next thing yah know they put me in the

Garage... The floor was cold and hard and it was a scary kind of dark in there. So I barked and whined as loud as I could. You figure they would let me back in... Right? Come on now! Is this any way to treat a guest?

That morning they left me alone in the garage all day! They even forgot to feed me and give me fresh water... Geez... What did I do? I didn't do anything wrong. SO I chewed a few things in the house. BIG deal. I was home all alone with nobody to play with. How was I supposed to know that you don't poo & pee in the house! What did they expected? As if I can hold it in ALL day. No dog can do that at any age, never mind a puppy. So a little time goes by, I start to get bigger, I'm still painfully cute, but just a little bigger. All of a sudden, they don't have any time for me anymore.

Well one hot sunny day, they didn't leave me any water or food. (Again) My stomach hurt really badly. I was so hungry I had to do something. So I was chewing on cabinet door where they hide my food. When all of a sudden, the man human comes home and catches me. Breaking & Entering with an intent to eat. The big dope starts yelling and screaming, waving his arms around. Like it's a crime to eat. Well, next thing I know, I'm sitting in the backyard chained up to a tree! Can you believe this guy! I was starving and just trying to get some food. I didn't do anything wrong. I might have chewed some shoes in the past. Maybe a slipper or two, But you can't eat Just one, Right...?

They left me out back seemed like all summer. I just spent every day, all day, by myself, alone and bored. I'd dig some holes in the ground or chase squirrels around to keep myself occupied but there's nothing to do. I can see the two of them coming and going ....I'd bark at them. Hey! Come play with me...Come give me some love....Every now and then, they let me come into the house, only to sit in a small cage in the corner. Boy, did I hate being in that cage.

Half the time I don't have any food or water. This is no way for a dog to live. I mean come on! Take me for a walk, take me for a ride in the truck, let's do something fun together! Life is supposed to be FUN...

Well the mean ole man human doesn't yelling at me as much as he used to. Now he just yells at the nice Lady human when she comes over to feed me. I don't even think she lives here anymore. Every now and then, she'll come out back and sit on the ground so she can talk with me. Salty water comes out of her eyes and I lick it from her face. That makes us both smile. Gosh, I hope that I'm not the reason he yells at her. He can be very mean, he even hit me with a stick one day. When I see him coming, I run and hide in the crappy ole dog house they got me ... The big Meany ...He can't get me in here. He tried to kick me in my butt once too. If that happens again, I'm going to turn around bite him in the Kester, see how he likes it. So this went on,

Seemed like forever. And she must've been bad, because I hear him screaming at her all the time. It's not my fault. But he keeps point his finger at me when he is yelling....

WELL...One-day-old Meany was yelling at the lady human! So I snuck out of my cage and squeezed out a smelly one, right where he sits at the table. Boy was he mad. The nice lady was opening the door at the time, so I bolted right outside. I ran down the street as fast as I could and I didn't dare look back. I ran until my paws were almost bleeding from the ruff road. I wanted so bad to get away from ole Meany, I was desperate. I did have a good laugh when I finally stopped running. But now, I didn't know what to do. I didn't know where I was. Nobody ever walked me around, I didn't know the area. I had NO idea what to do now. I didn't plan this. It just kinda happened. Then I saw this curly haired, sheep dog digging in some trash down the street.

I had nowhere to be. No plans for the rest of my life...So I went over and said Hey! Whatch yah doing? My name is Jayden. I am new to this area, can I hang out with you? Can you show me around the neighborhood? Well he told me his name is Jake and he would be more than happy to show me around town. My growling belly told him I was really hungry. So we dug in the trash together and found some old donuts to eat. After dumpster dining, we walked all around town and just talked and talked, just about life in general. He taught me a lot in the short time we were together. Jake had to go home once it got dark out. He lived with some nice humans on the upper west side of town. Funny, he didn't act like a yuppie puppy.

So here I am living on the streets. And for the past 10 days, I have been sleeping under cars and in alley ways, just to get out of the rain. I've been eating trash out of the garbage cans just to survive. When all of a sudden.... Woof... Ole

Meany was right in front of me! I tried to Run! But he was faster than I was. He pinned me to the ground hard. I struggled to get away. I growled ... Ouch! HEY... Don't touch me, not so ruff! I have rights yah NO! Well he didn't care. He just picked me up, and threw me in the back seat of the truck. He didn't seem too mad, at least he didn't hit me. Well, when we got back home, he took me straight to the backyard. Chained me up to the tree with no food, No water. Boy nice life huh...Well this went on for about two year's. I'd run away and ole Meany would come and find me...I wanted to get out of that place so bad!

Then one-day ole Meany walks up carrying my leash. I think he is going to take me for a walk. NO Way! I can't believe this. I'm going for a walk. WOOF! This is unreal....Woof... Better yet! I think we may be going for a ride in the truck! Hey, this is great! I never have been for a ride in ole Meany's truck. (Just back home when I escape) Oh wow! This is great. OH look. Hey, what's this? It says... I phone 8. Is this a chew toy? Crunch! Crunch! Crunch! Yuck, this isn't a toy! I'd better hide it before old Meany gets in. Oopps. Here he is….Hey! Can I drive? Hey Meany! Where are we going? Are we going to the Dog Park? Maybe I will see Jake. He said he gets to go to the park all the time. Boy this is fun. Can I stick my head out the window? Hey? This is awesome. How come you never did this with me before? This is fun…

What kind of Dog Park is this? It looks abandon. This can't be the dog park Jake told me about. He said his was brand new. So I don't think we are going to see him here. But either way, this is going to be great. It's about time you took me somewhere to play. Jeez, slow down! Let me smell some of the dog scents. I need to make some new friends… Woof…This place looks a little run down, almost haunted. And what's with the six foot fence. Looks more like a prison. I don't think we are in Yuppie Ville anymore…

Who is this guy wearing the fancy sunglasses? Hi Mister. Boy, you have a lot of dogs and cats. What do you do with all of them and why is everybody in a little cage? Hey! Meany! Where are you going now? You're not leaving me here! Are you? .You can't do this! I don't know anybody here! I'm scared! Don't Go! Hey! Specs... Stop him...! Please help me! Don't let him leave me here. I didn't do anything wrong .Why is he doing this to me? Hey Shades? Are you a friendly human? Because, I can't tell who is kind and who isn't. When I was an adorable little puppy, they loved me an always wanted to play with me. Now I can't even get them to feed me every day. How did things change so quickly? I don't understand.

Well you seem nice Shades. Do you have any food? Hey! What are you doing? What the heck! Hey! Put me down! What's going on? Bloop! Bloop! Bloop! What are you doing? Are you trying to drown me? ...Gurgle, gurgle, gurgle! What the heck. Do I look like a fish to you or something? Woof, Ohh... What's with all the bubbles? ....OHH...Hey...the waters nice and

warm, and the bubbles smell so sweet. Aahhh!
Woof! So relaxing. What's that goop you're
rubbing all over me? ...Uhmm...This feels kinda
cool on my coat, Hey! Buddy... can yah wash
behind my ears. I think I have a flea market
going on back there...Ohhhh... That feels sooo
good ...Hey a gal could get used to these bubble
baths. OH My Goodness. You're going to brush
me and comb my hair too...Woof... Nobody's ever
done this to me before. It hurts a little bit. But
Dam! I am looking mighty FINE again. I clean up
really Nice.... And I don't itch any more. This
must be the groomers Jake was telling me about.
I guess ole Meany isn't mean all the way thru
after all. I wonder when he is gonna come and
get me? This feels wonderful to be treated
humanely for a change. I am a still a little
surprised tho... Ole Meany must be up to
something, trying to be nice to me by getting me
groomed...Hey Foster Grants! Where are we
going now? OH sweet. We must be going for

walk....Hey look at all the other dogs. HI everybody. Boy this is great? Huh. Nice bubble bath and then a walk...   (Arff,Arff...Don't get used to it! girlie)

Woof. .. Hey! Which dog said that? Gee... What did he mean by that? Does he know something I don't know? Yo... Goggles... I thought we were going for a walk. What do you think you are doing? Don't be putting me in No cage fool. I am not staying in here. Ole Meany should be back soon. Hey! Where are you going now? HEY, don't turn out the lights! My human's coming back to get me? Really soon. Hey I didn't do anything wrong. Let me out of this cage! Oh great, now everybody's barking. WOW. It's loud in here! Great! How am I going to sleep with all this noise? I'm getting the feeling this isn't the fancy groomers Jake was telling me about! I hope my human comes back to get me soon... Tomorrow maybe? Even sitting in the backyard, all by myself, has got to be better than this...

Seems like I have been in here forever! Hey guys, what time is it? Better yet ...What day is it? Some nice man came and cleaned out my cage but he barely had time to talk to me. He didn't even pat me, rub my belly or anything. I don't think my human is ever coming back to get me. Well at least I have food every day. I don't have a flea circus living on my butt. Every now and then some nice humans come in after dinner and take me for a walk. The only good thing about being in here is, I've learned a lot from my K9 friends. Some of these dogs are really smart. I wonder what they did wrong to get in here. I feel funny asking them, because, I didn't do anything wrong. I just wanted to be loved, and have somebody I can love back. Why is that so hard to find in a human?

This isn't fair. How come nobody loves me? Those nice humans came an adopted Joe Boxer a couple of days ago. Why do I have to stay in here? I hate this little cage...Woof...Here's a nice family looking to adopt. Hey over here. Look at me. Down here! Hi everybody. Boy I am so happy to see you! I am glad you're adopting instead of buying a mill puppy... Hey guys! LOOK ... I think I'm getting some new humans. Two big ones, two small ones. I hope they treat me better than the last ones. OH NO! WAIT! WOOF! Where are you going? WOOF! HEY! Little boy. Don't go. I heard you say you wanted me! LOOK! Look! I can give you my Paw! I can sit pretty... HEY... little girl, tell your Daddy and Mommy to bring me home! HELP ME... Awww... Another family leaving without a dog.... Rejected again.

OH... Wait.... Hey, who is coming in now? It's a beautiful blonde woman and a tall handsome man. Hey! Hey! Over here! Pick me... Pick me... I'm down here...Woof.... I'm sooo happy to meet you. My name is Jayden...Look...I can sit...and give you my paw. Please take me for a walk. Please! Please. Oh my god! This is a good sign. She is going to get a leash. I hope they are going to take me for a walk, not that annoying little beagle next to me. I had better turn on the charm...Maybe they will take me home...HI... My name is Jayden. I'm sooo Happy to meet you. I'm a great watch dog, and I know not to chew things and I don't pee in the house. Who could ask for more... Will you take me home! Please. Oh please. At least take me for a walk. I'll show you around the Pen...OH, Ohh... Awesome, it is me. It's me this time...Yippee...Thank you. Thank you for picking me, come down here. Let me give you a kiss Blondie. Ohh... You smell lovely. Alrighty. Let's go for a long stroll and get to know one another. I haven't been walked in such a long time. Come on. Let's head down this way, the field is over here. Please stop pulling on my neck. I'm taking you for a tour of the Pen, Remember? Well then where do you want go? I'm willing to go anywhere you want ...

WOOF! We are going for a ride in your car? Super...This is really awesome. Wait until I tell the guys! They are gonna be Sooo jealous! Mind if I drive? Do you care if I move the seat and adjust the mirrors...woof .... Don't get pushy, I'm moving. You know I can't drive from back here,

Right? But that's okay, can I at least change the radio station? This is so exciting. So where do you wanna go? I don't know my way around here, so you're on your own. Boy this is one pimped out ride. Do you live in a bad neighborhood because somebody stole your roof? But this is kinda cool. Feeling the sun and the wind in my fur is amazing. It's like we are flying. This is Like, Totally Rad.... Sorry. Don't mind me. I babble like a broken bubbler when I get nervous...

Hey! Where we going? This is a colorful place. BK home of the Whopper. ..Yummy... I could go for a burger and fries. When I was living on the streets I dug a BK burger out of the trash... Yah... it was covered in coffee grinds and stuff. But when you're living on the streets, you eat what's available, or you don't eat....Woof...that was fast. Yah. Thanx Waldo...Check the bag. Make sure he gave us, napkins, salt & pepper. Good! Hey! Park in the shade over there. Don't forget! I'm wearing a fur coat, and your car doesn't have a roof... Thanks...

OK… Where's mine? You're not just going to sit there and eat that in front of me? I'll be nice and gentle, see, uummm… yummy! Thanks. Wow… This is great! Warm food. I've never had warm food before… What? Just one bite. Awww Come ON…Yeah I know it's not good for me, but neither is smoking and I saw you doing that earlier. Give it up! Come on Wimpy! Give me a bite of that burger. Oh yeah that's more like it. Hey! What do you have in the bag Blondie? Woof… What are these things called? Mmmm… Yummy… They are kinda salty. What's up with the red junk your putting all over them? I'm not too crazy about that Red stuff… but hey, food's food…Woof…That was SO tasty…I think I've died and gone to heaven.

Alrighty…Where are we going now? My friend Jake told me about a park where all the dogs get to run around and play together…Do you know where that is? Hey don't turn down here! Ohhh! I know where we are going. We are

going back to the PEN. Aren't we? Come on! PLEASE!
Please don't take me back to that place... Awww...
Please! I promise you I am a good girl. I wouldn't be
any problem at all. And I don't eat much. And I like to
play and jump around. LOOK! I know how to shake
paws. See, both of them, just not the same time. And
I've been told I'm a great kisser. Lick, Lick, Lick, Hey
Sugar, You taste a little salty! What's that coming out
of your eyes? Awww. We are back at this dump
already...

Hey Doll...Where is Fonzie going? Aaah... We
don't need him. I had one like him before, he used to
be mean to me, and would chain me up in the back
yard, alone, all day, with no food or water. Come on.
Hurry Let's GO! I'll drive. Give me the keys...Awww...
too late! Here he comes. Hey Jack, What's in the box?
...Woof... That's my old collar and my toys! Are you
taking me home? I can't believe it! I'm so happy! You'll
see, I'm going to be the best dog you ever had. I
learned all about caring for humans from all of my
pals in the pen. My job is security and I am the best at

it. I can't believe it. I am going to have a home to call my own ... WOOF... Where are we going? Ahhh ...It doesn't matter! The further away from the Pen the better. They say every dog has its day. Well. This must be mine...

Aw wait. I didn't get a chance to say good-bye to all my friends. Or to Specs, He was the gentlemen who took me in and gave me a flea bath and groomed me up pretty. He turned out to be a really nice guy .He really cared for the boys & girls that came to live with him. Every day he would come around and just sit with each one of us, talk to us, rub our bellies then give us a big hug. Even if it was only for a few seconds, he still took the time. I'm going to miss him the most. Woof. This is a long ride. I'm kinda feeling a little woozy. I'm not used to riding in the car for so long.

Hey...What's this place we are pulling into? C.V.S... Hey Lady. Where is Stretch going? That's

alright. I'll just sit here in talk to you, Baby! Hey look
out. Who's this guy? Woof! Woof! Woof ! ... YAH...
Grrrrrr... Oh that's right buddy. Back off Jack! WOOF!
WOOF! She's mine... I'll rip your hands off... That's
right you had better get away from her. Woof! ...

Aww, cutie pie. What's with the hugs and kisses.
Oh, did I do a good job? All I did was chase that bad
guy away. Hey... Slim. You're back so soon. Hey. Let me
tell you what I did! I chased away a bad guy. Yah. He
stuck his hand in the car and was trying to get us, so I
told him to...oof... Alright, Easy...Don't hug me so
hard...I was just doing my job. Ok, here is a kiss for you
too. Lick, lick, Lick ... Boy oh boy...It doesn't take much
to make you two happy. Ahhh look! Sugar plumb has
got that salty water coming from her eyes again. Lick,
lick, and it tastes kinda good. That's a pretty slick
trick. How about a little less salt tho... I'm trying to
watch my sodium intake. SO Hey! You think I can drive
now? Ohhh... all right, I'll just sit back here and looking
pretty...

Isn't this turning out to be a great day? I got myself some new humans, a nice car to ride in, no more smelly cages or crazy barking dogs. Don't get me wrong, I will always love all of my friends that I made in the pen, and I love to bark too! But I just like to have a reason. That was such a noisy, smelly place. I'm not gonna miss it one bit.

Woof... Are we here? Is this my new home? ... Woof... This is a nice place. It's enormous! Wow, smell all the different smells. I can smell squirrels and raccoons. All sorts of dogs walk by here too. I don't know. I'm getting a little scared! This place is kinda big for me to protect. Joe Boxer told me that to be a good dog, I have to protect the house. Joe was my first friend at the pen. He was one cool dude. A little crazy though. He got booted from his house for eating a couch. I mean come on! Who eats a couch? Right... I peed on the couch once at Ole Meany's house. Boy was he mad! He chase me down the street with a stick. He never did catch me though. I didn't come home for 3 days. It was raining and I was cold, but I didn't care! I don't like getting hit because it stings for days. Well. I think he forgot about it once I came home. He locked me out in the back yard, and he didn't come out to get me for days. I was cold and hungry but you know what? It's better than being hit by a stick...Woof... Sorry... I am babbling again. I'm still a little nervous about this ...

Here Jayden... here's your new home... come on girl... yea, yea! Okay! I'm coming I'm coming. Just smelling this yellow and red plug you have out front. Wow you have a lot of dog friends. Where are they? ...Woof... This place isn't another dog Pen is it? I don't see any cages. All right, all right. Here I come. Just let me sign my name to the guest list first... Ok I'm done ...Here I come...WOOF ...

This is a nice place! Is this all mine? Hey! I smell cats. Are they still living here? Because we don't get along. AT ALL....

Ohhh my God....This place is huge. This Pad is totally awesome. Woof... Look at this room. I love what you've done with it. The fire place, the hardwood floors ... WOOF... That's a nice leather chair. Hey Baby cakes, Can I sit up here in the window sill? ...Awww... Thanx, and would ya look at this view! OH Boy. When I sit up here, I can see everything out side. I don't even care what the rest of the place looks like. I can run my entire security operation from up here. Roger That!

WOOF! Woof! Hey you! Hey get out of my yard. Woof, Woof... Hey! Blondie. Look out! We've got Burglars already. Here they come. They are going to the side door. Don't worry! I got this. WOOF! WOOF! WOOF! Get off my property or your dead meat! WOOF... Hey quit pulling on my neck. I can handle this. OH! So you know these hoodlums? Wait let me smell them first. Alright, file in, one at a time. One at a time please. Let me take a sniff first...WOOF! Stop right there granny! You smell like a cat! It's not in your purse, is it? Well... Ok you can go in. Just leave any cats you have with you outside. Ok! Next. Hey Smiley! You smell like a cat too! And you smell like one too, Lurch. Hey! What is this? A cat convention! Doesn't anybody smell like a dog? OHH wait! This one smells like a dog! Woof.... She also smells like 1, 2 sniff, sniff...3 maybe 4 cats! Are you "cat woman"? All right come on in. BUT I'm keeping my eye on this one, leave your cats outside!

Woof... All right. TAKE it Easy...Easy, don't everybody pat me all at once! You're freaking me out! I've never been treated so nice. {Hey a dog could get use to this.} So who are you people? Do you live here? Or did you just come to see me? ...Woof. ..Hey you! Blondie! Yes you. What's your name? Yeah you! I'm talking to you Sugar plumb. What's your name? You never did tell me your name. And who are all these cat smelling humans? *Bla Bla Bla...* I don't know what that means.... You don't speak dog, do you? Boy. She's not too bright, but she sure is sweet and sometimes salty. Okay, I guess I will just call you Mommy. What is that in your hands Mommy? Yah...sure, I will have some water. Of course I will have some bacon treats. Bacon treats rule! Yeah!

Woof! Hey there you are Moose. I was looking for you. Look! Mommy gave me some Bacon treats. Mmmm, yummy, you want one? I don't mind sharing. Sharing is good. I got the feeling these humans don't talk too much dog. I guess I'm gonna have to teach them. Hey Moose. Ya you. Tall dark and handsome. Hey I'm going to call you Daddy! Okay? So when I say (Daddy). You come running! Okay? Because that mean's somebody's at the door, and I need you... Woof... You're not too sharp either. This is going to be like cutting steak with a rubber knife. Oh well. I'm going to play with these feline lovers for a little while. I'll do my best to turn them into DOG lovers. I kinda like all the affection. It's nice to be the center of attention again. It's been a long time since I've felt loved and had somebody to love back. It sure is heartwarming...

Woof! Daddy, the stray cat family tuckered me out chasing the ball. Jeepers' creepers. I thought they were never going to leave…Woof… I'm so tired! I need a nap. I could fall asleep right here at Mommy's feet. This entire day has been more like a dream… I hope I never wake up…

WOOF…What the! Where am I? What's going on? Holy smokes. I did get adopted. I thought I was dreaming. Good morning Mommy, Good morning Daddy, What happened? Did I fall asleep on the job? I'm sorry but the crazy cat family that came over yesterday, just wore me out, so Daddy. Are you going to tell me who they were? Or should I just bark at everybody? Yo! Daddy I'm talking to you. Don't you see my tail wagging and the look on my face? This is going to be tough getting thru to these two. Oh never mind… I'll just bark at everybody….

Hey Daddy! Where are we going? Awesome we are going for a ride. YAH…Let's GO! Hey…This is one nice rig. Is this my truck? Wow. I got this. Its high but I can jump up. Hey throw me the keys. Easy! Don't push... don't push... Are you gonna let me drive this thing or what? I AM head of security. All right! I'll just sit over here and look pretty. Yee ha! This is awesome Daddy! Where we going? All right don't answer me! I'll just stick my head out the window and enjoy the ride.

Stop! ... Stop! I just saw a squirrel. Oh shucks! You went right by him. I can't stand squirrels Daddy. They use to steal my food when I was little. They would take it and put it up in the tree, worse of all, they would laugh at me, because I couldn't get to it,   I was all alone... and I never knew when I would get more food. And I was Woooo! HEY! Tell me when we're gonna stop like that! You almost put me thru the windshield and turned me into a Pug at the same time. That's it Mario! I'm driving!

Woof... What is this place? Looks like a big Old barn...Hey Daddy! Can I come in? Woof...

Alright! Cool, give me a minute. I got to fix my hair. "Shake" "shake ""shake"... OK...I am ready... Let's go. Wow! This place is something else? WOW! Look at all the dog food, piled up to the sky. Can you smell all the different food's Daddy? Dog food, cat food, rabbit pellets, bird food! FOOD! Food! ... Everywhere! ... Oh my goodness. I've never seen so much food in all my life. ?

Woof... What the heck is that? Looks like a goat. Now who would bring a goat to the city? Oh look... Rabbits let me get 'em... Alright! Alright! Quit yanking my chain. I wouldn't touch them. Ok, cut me some slack, I've got more things to smell. Hey Limbaugh, what's the Rush? Slow down...

Hey Daddy, What's that on your shoulder? Oh sweet! A giant bag of DOG food. Hey that one over there smells better. NO, I'm not complaining. I'll eat anything. Any dog food is better than going hungry! It's better than getting your dinner out of the garbage pail too. Hahhh! Been there, done that, Ate the tee shirt. One time I got ahold of something spicy. Taste good going down. Burns like heck coming out the tail end, if you know what I saying. How do you humans eat stuff like that? Hey where are yah going? I'm not done looking around yet...Ok ...Ok... I'm coming...

Hey Daddy! Where are we going now? Can I stick my head out the window? Okay, well can you put down the window for me please? I don't know how too. I haven't driven in one of these fancy trucks before. So are you going to tell me where we are going? Or do I have to guess? Ok... Is it the groomers? Because, I could use a Pedi and a Mani. I heard that was a Hip and Happening place to hang out. Maybe we will see Jake.

Woof...What's this place? WOW, Check out the ginormous fields of grass! And look at all the super huge trees. You know what that means? Squirrels! Can I chase the squirrels Daddy? Can

I? Can I? Can I? Park right over there. Come ON! Hurry! Hurry...I'm SO excited. This is totally awesome. I've never been to a huge park like this. I've just heard stories in the pen. Hurry! Let's GO! Put the phone away. Can't you see how bad I want to go? Well let's Move it...

Woof...It's about time. Well you have to take the leash off me! Because most squirrels are fast. Oh Ok, You're going to chase them with me! Okay...Hurry up! Let's go! Let's move it Daddy! This way! This way! You've got to pick up the pace. Because we are not going to catch any at this rate! Okay...OK .Quit pulling on my neck. Fine... I'll slow down. But don't blame me when we don't catch any squirrels.

WOOF... This place is like a dream I had once. For a long slow walk, I sure am tired. Can you pick me up and put me in the truck Daddy? I think I pulled a muscle. I haven't run around so much since I ran away from Big Ole Meany. If I fall asleep, wake me up when we get home Daddy ...Thanks Daddy "Kissy " "Kissy "

I had a great time today Daddy..."Lick " "Lick " "
Lick " " I won't tell Mommy it's your fault we
didn't catch any squirrels.   " Nuzzle, Nuzzle " I
had so much fun today. I love you Daddy!

Hey we're home already? There's Mommy.
MOMMY! MOMMY! Guess what we did? We went,
and got a hefty sack of dog food at the Old barn,
and I saw a goat, and some rabbits, and then we
went to this park. It was humongous! It had lots
and lots of grass and a forest full of trees, and a
whole mess of squirrels to chase. But Ssshhh....
I'm not supposed to tell you, but Daddy is slow!
We didn't catch any squirrels! But that's okay.
Boy O Boy! Am I tired. I pulled Daddy all around
that place... Thank You Daddy...

I had the best time of my whole life! "Kiss
""Kiss" "Kiss "... Geez... I am exhausted. I'll be
right here in the window, if you need me.

I'm so beat...My legs hurt from all the
walking and chasing squirrels. I must be out of

shape from sitting in that stupid cage all that time. This is like a dream come true. One day, I'm so hungry, with nobody to talk to, I am out in the cold. I've got flea market working overtime on my butt. Then I get discarded to the pen like I'm yesterday's trash. NOW! I've got new humans and a nice house to protect and they seem to really like me a lot. But then again, the old humans were nice to me for a little while too. After time ... It was like they didn't even want me around. I had better pay closer attention next trip to that old barn. They had food piled up to the sky. If I do have to run away, I will run to the barn. At least I won't go hungry. WHY am I even thinking like this? I'm sure Mommy and Daddy wouldn't do to me, what the bad humans did to me. I'd hate to run away again. It's awfully scary being out there in the world, all by yourself.

Life sure is flying by here at my new Mommy and Daddy's house. The days were so long and lonely out in the backyard at Ole Meany's place. I hope I never see them again. I heard the truck. I think Mommy and

Daddy are home. Look, they have a pine tree with them. Maybe it's for me to pee on. Hey Mommy. Hey Daddy. What's with the pine tree? Where are you going with it? You're not bringing that in the house, are you? What are you going to do with it? Better yet. Where are you going to put it?

HEY! Don't be moving my chair. Hey! I need to sit on the window sill to see. You're forgetting! I'm only two feet tall. How can I protect you if I can't see whose coming? Hello! I'm talking to you. Yeah it's me down here.... AWWW... Forget it! I'm going to sleep in THEIR bedroom, if they're going to mess with MY bedroom....Your putting your life in danger without security, Ya kno?

Woof... Where did everybody go and where is my chair? OK, I see it, tucked in the corner over there. What's with all the bright lights on this tree? How am I gonna see out the window now? How am I gonna do my job? Oh they are gonna hear about this! First thing in the morning...

MOMMY! DADDY! **Somebody broke in while I was sleeping. I mean, uhm, while I was on duty! And umm, it happened so fast. I'm sorry! I didn't even see them. I didn't get a chance to bite them or anything! Umm...Let's see... I think they may have come in thru the chimney. Cuz look, their red stockings are stuck on the fireplace mantle. Let me take a closer look. Stand back now, it could be a trap! Haaa...That's funny. The big stocking smells like Bacon bits and the two on the end smell like chocolate. HEY! Is somebody s playing a trick on me? What's going on? Hey look at all the pretty boxes under the pine tree. I wonder what's in them? Sniff sniff... Nothing I've ever smelled before. Good morning Mommy... What's for breakfast? I can smell something good cooking...Woof... LOOK! I got something in my bowl. Yummy...Oh Boy that was good! Bacon & eggs with home Fries. I wonder, what's the special occasion?**

Woof. Hey Daddy! We've got intruders...WOOF... Let me att'em. Who are all these people coming in the house? Help Daddy. They are all coming in at once...HELP....Where did they all come from. They all want to pet me at once. Hey. I love attention... but... like...this is creepy! That's it I'm out of here. Hey! There is my leash, maybe if I push around with my nose, somebody will notice. Hey you. What's your name? You look like my Mommy wearing glasses. Please! TAKE ME FOR A WALK! Get me out of here! Too many people all at once. I'm getting stepped on down here... Woof... Alrighty... She speaks dog. Thanks for get me out of there sweet heart. All of those little humans came out of nowhere. I thought I was being attacked by a ten armed mini monster...

Ahhh Feel the cool fresh air...Hey Madonna... Where are you going? We walk down this way... Woof... You humans. Okay! We can go your way, but if you get lost, you're on your own.

My nose doesn't work well with all this white stuff on the ground. Speaking of this white stuff, Let me tell you what my bad humans did to me. They left me outside chained to a tree while this white stuff fell out of the sky. It fell ALL DAY! I was nearly buried alive. I think that was about two years ago, maybe three. They were SO mean. So I kept shaking & shaking to keep it off of me. BOY was I cold... Woof... Wait...Let's stop. I got some business to take care of. I hope you brought a little pink bag with you, because for some strange reason, they like to save it. Don't ask me what they do with it. Cuz I don't know, and I Don't wanna know... OK... I'm done. Ohhh yaaa, that's a keepah! Give that one to Mommy, she can put it with the rest of them.

Woof ... We might as well go back and get this over with! Nobody better have laid a finger on my bacon filled stocking! I don't feel like hurting anybody today. Boy o boy...it's freezing out here... Woof... speaking of Cold. I was telling you about the day I was left out side in this stuff. Can you imagine somebody doing that to me? Why would anybody be so mean to me? I just wanted somebody to take care of me and Love me...I don't understand a lot of what you humans do. I'm just sooo happy I have a new loving family ...Woof... Let's go back home. I'm getting hungry...

Hey...We're back! I'm all wet. You may want to stand back, I'm going to Shake Rattle & Roll! Just like the king... Hey Elvis. I told you to stand back. Awww...Did I get you wet...ha ha...you're not gonna melt big boy. OH Great, more humans that can't speak dog!

Boy o boy...It's gonna be a job in itself, training all these bananas'. Holy smoke! Even more people came when I was out walking. Hey! Watch it. You stepped on my paw. I'm okay! I know you didn't mean it. Why is it so crowded in here? Must be all the food. I think I'm gonna high tail it to the living room...

Hey! Ole man... How's it going? Woof! Hey, don't smack me! Oh yea, you want to play, Huh...

Arrrr... Grr, Grr ,Grrr. Ha ha.... look out. Watch this. Ha ha. I call it my burn out. Wooo...Yee haa... around and around I go. Weeee... Look out now! Hey that floor is slippery. Alright you got me. Ha ha... Aww. Big hug...Kiss Kiss... Hey! Your all right pops..! That was fun! Gee. What's that on your plate? Smells good? Yeah sure. I'll try some. Thanks. Hey watch out! Here comes Mommy. HEY! Mommy! I was eating that! That was good too. What was that? Jeez...Mommy... Hey Gramps, what was that? Man that was delicious! Why did Mommy take it away? Pssst hey. When she's not looking, give me some more. Will ya, puh-leez? I promise not to tell on you. Thanx Pops. You're the MAN.....

Hey, where's everybody going? We are all going to sit down and eat. Alright, where's my chair? Awww, come on. How come I don't get to sit up there with all the food? Ohhh...alright. I'll be down here. Hey Pops! Drop something for me, will ya.... Hey...all right...I got it... I got it. Boy that was delicious. I think? I don't know. I swallowed it so fast. I don't even know what it

was. But it sure tasted good. Hey Gramps, drop
some more of that when Mommy's not looking.
Will ya? ...

Woof ...That was a great meal! Everybody
dropped a little something, and Mommy was so
busy, she didn't see a thing. I'm stuffed. Dam, a
girl could lose her figure if she's not careful.
So...What's for dessert?

All right, now where is everybody going?
Okay let's all go back into the living room. Why is
everybody staring at the crazy box of lights on
the wall? You better not be looking at my bacon
filled stocking. What the... Now everybody
screaming at the crazy light Box! Why are they
yelling at the box, RUN... and ...GO PATS! Boy
these humans are crazy. I think I'll see if Mommy
with glasses wants to go for a walk again and
chase some squirrels, I don't have the heart to
tell her. I think I chased them all away. Because I
haven't seen a squirrel since all of this cold

white stuff fell. I just see a lot of little flying things. They go up to that little wooden box over there, hanging in the tree. I've tried, but I can never catch them. They jump up in the air, flap their arms and away they go...I tried to do that once. But I fell on my head, so I don't even try anymore. Besides, their food doesn't taste that good at all! They dropped a few little dried out pieces of junk on the ground. So I tasted it one day, yuck! They can have it, it's for the birds...

Hey, you, Mommy with glasses...Yah ...I am talking to you, let's go for a walk down the street. Yah, yah, grab the leash. Alright let's go...hurry! Hurry! You See that... I knew she could speak a little dog talk. Thanx for getting me out of there. Let's go this way. Come over here, I want to show you a few things. Do you see under there? There is a black cat with a white stripped tail. He lives under this camper, and boy does HE needs a lesson in hygiene..... He squirted me one day, Right in the face. I stunk so badly, Mommy and Daddy had to give me a bath in this smelly red stuff. I don't know what smelled worse. The red junk or me.

Well.... They gave me a bath 2 or 3 times that day. So if you see that black stink bomb with a white stripe, don't hang around and ask a lot of questions, just run... Woof... I don't see him much this time of year. Hey! Mary Poppins. Are you paying attention? Come on. Let's go down the street, this way Miss daisy...

See that house over there? They have a dog, I call her Lucy. She doesn't say much. I don't think they are very nice to her. They leave her outside all day by herself. I hear her crying all the time, even when she is in the house, I can hear her, she just cries and cries. I left her my ham bone one day. She was really thankful. I try and talk to her and teach her things, so maybe her humans will be nicer to her. She is always so sad. I never know what to say. I wish she could come live with us... My Mommy & Daddy would be so nice to her. Give her a bath and a flea dip, then maybe she wouldn't be so sad. But I'm not too sure I would like sharing my Mommy &

Daddy. But I've spent a long time living like that, and it's NO FUN! I hope they don't bring her to the pen .She wouldn't like it there either.

Alright ...it's getting cold out here, my paws are soaked and it's making me chilly. Let's head back. Come this way, Ok look out, me first. I gotta check things out, make sure it's safe. Cause that's my job. Mommy and Daddy need my protection ya know? They always tell me what a good job I do. And they buy me presents. I've got some pretty ones under the tree in the house. I'll show them to you when we get back...

HEY everybody... We're back. I'm A COLD & WET DOG. SO. Look out! I am gonna SHAKE... Here we go... SHAKE... shake... SHAKE. Woohoo, That floor is slippery. Whoosh. Look out! Coming through. Hey, that's kind of neat. Everybody moves out of the way because I'm all wet. Ha ha ha. What a bunch of wimps! They could never stay outside like I did. Chained up to a tree, in the cold, in the rain, in the snow. I did it for years, not just a few days. Alright. Spread out. Coming

through. I think I'll sit over here near the
fireplace and dry out a little bit. I'm happy to see
nobody touched my bacon filled stocking. I'd
hate to bite someone on such a festive day. Ah
this is the life. I've got myself a nice pack of
humans. I think I'll keep them around for a
while. I gonna put my head down and rest for a
second. My neck hurts from pulling Mommy with
glasses around the block. She is really nice to
me, just like my Mommy.

Woof...! Where did everybody go? I must
have fallen asleep .BOY oh Boy. That was a long
day! Mommy? Daddy? Where are you? Nobody is
awake. They must be in the bedroom. Yup...
There you are. I wonder what it's like to sleep
way up there on the bed? I'll jump up there
someday. I better not do it today tho, I'll do it
when nobody's around...

Hey Mommy, Hey Daddy, It's about time
you woke up! I've been sitting in the kitchen

staring at this door for hours. I almost pee'd my pants! And I don't even wear pants! SO. Let's go! Let's go! You gotta hurry or we're gonna have a mess on our hands! I'm talking major flooding with possible mud slides. I'm sorry, but when you gotta GO! You gotta GO!

I think I may have licked up too many spilt drinks off the floor yesterday. I'm never gonna do that again. I hope you grabbed your coat! I've got a feeling we're going to be outside for a while…. come on let's move! There's going to be a flood! Hurry!

Ahhhh… I feel better now. We can go back home now. We don't have to walk all the way around the block. It's artic cold out today. Hey Mommy. I got one question for you .WHY do you keep my poop in a little pink bag? It's not like its valuable or anything. Because I got news for yah! There is a whole lot more where that came from! You just bring the Ole guy over, he's got food in his pockets that'll make this stuff shoot right out of you, as soon as you eat it. I gotta learn to lean in and sniff a little bit first before woofing down anything he gives me. Cuz ya never know what Houdini is going to pull out of his pocket. He always has something for me tho. I like him, he treats me nice. He is a good human ...I just gotta stay away from his spicy treat's. Mommy, I think I'll take nap near the fire place when we get home...

Ahaah ... This is the life! Not many people walking by the house to bark at. We got this cold white stuff on the ground. (Daddy calls it snow). My life is simple, just eating, sleeping and taking my humans for a walk every now and then. ...Woof...This is the way all dogs should live!

Oh Hey! What is going on? Where did all you humans come from? I've been sleeping down stairs. I didn't see you coming in. What the... Looks like a party to me? There is that drunk guy with the lamp shade on his head again. Who is this guy? Hey what are you eating chief? That looks good can I have some? WOW... everybody looks pretty fuzzy to me... Woof... It's crazy loud out here. Worse than the pen, on a full moon. How did I sleep through this? I must be losing my hearing...Woof... What the heck is going on NOW? 10... 9...8 ... Why is everybody screaming? 7....6...5 Will somebody tell me what the heck is going on? 4...3...2...1...

HAPPY NEW YEAR...!!

Wholly cow! It's loud out here. HEY! Get your nose off of my mommy's nose. This is out of control! Everybody yelling and singing and rubbing noses ...I AM OUT OF HERE....You bunch of bananas can let your selves out. I am going back down stairs to sleep. Sometimes you humans are just plain CRAZY..!

Mommy! Daddy! Where are you? Hurry up! I got to go out. Awww man. I can't wait. Oh NO! I made a mess on the floor, oh man, I'm in big trouble now. I'd better hide! Last time this happened, I got hit with a stick by the Ole Meanie. Oh No. There's Mommy. I'm sorry Mommy. I didn't mean it. It will never happen again! Don't hit me with a stick, Please. I held it as long as I could. If I could, I would have put it in one of those little pink bags. Oh NO! She's coming at me. I'm sorry Mommy. Please don't hit me. What? She patting me on the head and she saying something, NOW she's giving me a bacon treat. I don't get it.

Woof ... Thanks Mommy. That was weird! No stick! No yelling! No hitting. And she gave me a treat to boot. This is crazy! One human hit's you with a stick! Another human gives you a treat and pats you on the head for doing the same thing. Hey... I'm not complaining. Just confused???

Hey Mommy! Where are you going? I'm sorry you had to clean up my mess so early. Are you going back to bed? Yeah! I think I could use a nap myself. I licked up something off the floor that was spilt and I am not feeling too good. I'm feeling kinda fuzzy myself, a little run down.

Alrighty then. I'll be sitting in the window if you need me. Mommy didn't look too good. I think she had too much fun last night. I was gonna take her for a walk. But I didn't want to push my luck. That stuff they drink makes you crazy. But they all seemed to be having fun. They sure were a loud bunch. I'm glad they only do that once a year...

Good morning Daddy. Where are we going so early? We're going for a cruise in the truck.   Alright let's go. Holy cow! Where did all this snow come from? Boy it is deep. All Righty Daddy. Let's go get; em! Yee ha Daddy! Ride em cowboy... smash into that white stuff!

This is a crazy kinda fun, but how long do we have to smash into this white stuff? Seems like we've been out here all day, and I'm not feeling too good. You're looking kind of purple yourself. Yeah. Good Idea. Let's pull over for a while. We can get out of here and stretch our legs. ...Woof... What are you doing Daddy? Why are you spitting out your lunch? Hey I'll eat that. Alright! Alright! I'll get back in the truck, but that was some good chow you threw away. Alright, I'll shut up. Sorry Daddy. Hey! You don't look so good .You kinda got this ghostly glow to your face. Maybe we should go home. I'm not even gonna ask to drive, let's Just go...

MOMMY! Daddy's not feeling very good, I know because he threw away his lunch and didn't even let me have it, now he looks like a smurf. Maybe you could make us a sandwich or something warm. It's cold out. And it's a lot of work smashing the snow around in the truck. I think that's why Daddy is sick, we do a lot of bouncing around. I don't like being banged around either. But I just love being with Daddy in the truck. ...Woof... I am gonna check the house for intruders, then go to sleep in my window. Good night Daddy. I hope you feel better. Thanx for taking me with you. I just love hanging out with Daddy. He needs me to protect the truck when he leaves it for a little while. I always get a treat, or a bite of his sandwich for doing a good job. He is a good boss to work for...

Boy OH Boy. It sure has been a long winter. It's finally getting a little warm out during the day. I just been sleeping, eating and taking Mommy for short walks. I can't walk all the way around the block any more. I get tired and have to sit down. As a matter of fact. I think I'll take a nap right now. Mommy is cooking my favorite today. Corned beef with potatoes & carrots and some smelly green stuff that makes Daddy fart. A LOT!!! And Holey Moley does he stink! The black cat with the white stripe smell like roses compared to him. Then he always tries to blame me. I don't even like the green stuff. I just eat the meat & potato... I think I will cuddle up on the couch. Nobody is using it. I need to take a rest from sitting in the window, watching for intruders. Things are pretty slow when it's cold out...

Hey, what's going on out here? How did everybody sneak in here without me seeing them? I'm gonna have to get my hearing checked. Woof, And why are they all wearing green clothes? Hey, there is that guy with the lamp shade on his head. And there's that skinny guy that keeps laughing all the time. Boy are these humans crazy And they're all talking so loud I'm going back to the kitchen. I think I smell the corn beef that Mommy was cooking earlier. It should be done by now! What's with this schmuck? He's dropping more food than he's getting in his mouth. I think I'll follow him around for a while. He's dropping some good stuff. Maybe I'll go take a nap downstairs after I clean up after this sloth. Because, it's way too loud up here for me...

Boy... time sure is flying by living with Mommy and Daddy...They have been so nice to me, every single day. They never hit me or yell at me. Mommy buys me toys every time she goes some place. They even got me a dead squirrel to practice with. He makes a loud squeaking noise every time I bite him, I have been running around the house with him trying to show everybody. Daddy keeps throwing him into the other room and I keep bringing him back. It's kind of boring, but if it makes Daddy happy, I'll keep doing it. Sometimes I just gotta pretend I can't find it. And walk away, otherwise he would do this all day...

Sometimes I think he's Lost IT. He's got me chasing my tail around in circles and then laughs at me when I fall down. Like I'm the crazy one. Well, if that's all it takes to keep him entertained it's the least I can do. After all, he did save me from the Pen. And it sure beats sitting outside in the rain with nobody to talk too, with NO food or water. Sometimes I think I'm living in a dream world, and I will wake up, all by myself again, cold and hungry. Somebody pinch me! This is too good to be true. It makes me wonder how all the guys and girls are doing at the Pen. I hope they found some nice humans to love them and care for them, sweet and kind, like my mommy & daddy.

Well it sure is getting warm out the past few months. Mommy, why are you making all of this food? Can I go in the backyard? I've got business to take care of. Just open the door, I won't run away. I Promise. Thanx. All right now! This has got to stop! How did all these humans get in the backyard without me seeing them? And why are they all dressed in red white and blue...

Woof... Hey! Who are you? Have you been here before? Don't you know I'm head of security? Come over here let me smell you...sniff, sniff... Okay you can go, but check in with me next time you come in my yard. How about the rest of these Blokes... This is way too much to ask. I can't possibly keep an eye on all these humans. I may need some help from one of my friends at the Pen. I've smelled most of these people before, but I've got some new ones to keep an eye on. It's funny some of them smell a little like Daddy, some of them smell like

Mommy...Just a different kinda smell, but the same, does that make sense?

Woof... Hey. There's the ole guy that keeps food is pockets. Let's go see what he's up to...Hey Pops! How's it going? What do you have for me? Anything good? Ohoo yeah, I'll take some of that chicken ... Gulp, Gulp... (Gone) Ok Thanks I have to run, I just saw somebody drop a hamburger.... I'll be back tho, save the chicken knuckles & skin for me. Thanx gramps.

Man o man, I've never eaten so much in my life. Where did everybody go? I must have fallen asleep. Now everybody's gone, even Mommy and Daddy. Boom ! What the..... Bang Boom Bang! Hey who's doing that? Stop it... Boom, bang , boom! Stop it! Please! That's hurting my ears! Boooommmmm! Bang! Boom! That's it I'm getting out of here. I'm going downstairs in the cellar. Boom...bang.... Ohhh my God, this can't be happening! Mommy! DADDY! Help... I'm SCARED... BOOM... ... bang...boom ... Bang...boom.... well it's not as loud down stairs under the bed...Boom Bang Boom ...

OH my god, I thought that would never stop. I think I'll stay here for a little while longer. Woof. Hey Mommy! Hey Daddy! Boy! I'm glad to see you made it back alive! What was going on out there? Sounded like bombs were going off. I was so scared there were all these LOUD noises, it was hurting my ears and the whole house was shaking. I think I even pee'd myself. but ...uummm.... that didn't stop me from doing my job. Uum ... umm... Well...You see, the noise was coming from under the bed. I looked under there for a while but I didn't find anything, and then it finally stopped. So I quit looking, everything's secure down here! You can count on me! Hey Mommy! Can I sit with you for a little while? I want to tell you how brave I was...

Woof... It sure is getting hot out. Oh, Hey Daddy. Oh. You want to go for a ride in my truck. OK! Let's go... Boy I love tooling around in this truck... Hey ...Daddy can I drive? Ah come on I'm sitting right here! .... Alright... alright.... don't get pushy. I am head of security. I should have my own truck. Hey can you push that button right there. Yeah, that one. All right, Thanks. Ahhh, Cool air, right in my face. Ah, that feels good. I am wearing this thick heavy fur coat. This sure beats digging a hole in the backyard, and lying in it to stay cool. Ahh, this is the life, tooling around in my truck, Music cranked up, Air conditioner on high. Ahhh Life is good....

Hey! What's this place we are pulling into? Daddy, can you put the window down! It gets awfully hot in here without the A.C turned on. My bad humans left me in the car one day with no water! And the windows were up all the way. I almost passed out. Oh I can come in with you. That's great. I like going to new places.... Oh No! I smell a lot of dogs. I hope this isn't another dog pound... Awhhh man... Here we go again! I knew it! I knew it! Things were going way too good to be true.... That's it I'm out of here... woof... Easy on the neck!

Hey, who is this guy? Hey Baldy...Don't try to be nice to me.... I know what's going on Daddy! Daddy! Don't leave me! I didn't do anything wrong! Daddy come back. Oh no, Here we go again. What is this place? I don't see any cages... woof... Hey! Put me down! What are you doing? You're getting me all wet... NO.... I don't want any treats I told you...Back off ...Don't try to be nice to me... Oh No. This guy thinks I'm a fish, just like when I got dropped off at the Pen... I don't believe this!! I've been double crossed! I've been doing my job for Mommy and Daddy! And this is the thanks I get... listen buddy I don't care how nice you are to me. Pat me! Rub my belly all you want! I am sick and tired of this. I am running away the first chance I get! Maybe I can find that big barn with the huge piles of food... I do not need these humans anymore. Hey! What is that noise?

Bbbuuzzzzz... zzz.z.z .z.z.z.z.z...zzz! Get that thing off of me! What the ... Hey stop that!

Bzzzz... Hey! That's my fur on the ground. WHAT are you doing? Oh you're gonna pay for this buddy! Bzzz ... Why, I'm going to...Hey! You know what? That doesn't feel too bad. Oh yeah, my hind legs feel free again. Ohhh yeah...Awww. That's nice! I can move my hind legs, with no fur pulling on my skin. Now I can bite those fleas better too, but you know what? I don't feel them anymore. Hey, Kojack. Will you take a little bit off the top and don't forget my tail section. Oh yeah that feels good. Hey! Where are you going with all my fur? I may need that back! I may be sleeping outside again. That would make a warm little bed. OOHH... This guy is stealing the fur off my back. You just can't trust any humans.

Oh my god! Daddy! Daddy! You came back for Me.! ... I thought you were leaving me here! Look at me Daddy, I am naked and I smell like a human. But I am so happy you came back for me... Wahoo ...Watch me spin around yee haa ... hey, Hey! What are you laughing at? Daddy it's me! ... Quit laughing ...OH... So you think this is funny? Alright! Let's go home... When we get home, you are in big trouble! I am telling Mommy you laughed at me..... Yeah! See you later Mr. Clean... Thanks for nothing! Look at what you did to me! Daddy can't stop laughing at me. Come on, let's go! And wipe that smirk off your face! Or I will chew up your slippers again...

Ahh... Here we are. Home at last. Boy that was a close one. I thought I was a goner. Mommy, Mommy There you are! Look at what the bald guy did to me! ... Oh so you're going to laugh too? Hey, this isn't funny! .... I was scared! ....

I thought you were getting rid of me, like the Mean humans did. Dropping me off and not coming back. Alright! Would you two stop laughing! Enough is enough. I've been through a lot of stress today. Well if you too can't stop laughing at me, I'm going to take a nap in the window...

Oh no. Here she comes. Hey Mommy, No, I'm not mad at you, but when Daddy drop me off there, I got scared. The bald guy was very nice to me... He tried to give me a snack and everything. but I was busy thinking of a way to get out of there. Yeah you're right. I do feel much cooler, and the fur on my behind is not pulling on my skin. And he evicted the flea market too... Thank you Mommy. (Kiss) (Kiss) I'm not mad at you... Do I really look that funny? Cause I feel kinda sexy...woo woo. :)

Mommy! Mommy! Quick, Hurry! Let me out. There is a handsome boy in our back yard. I smelled him earlier, boy is he adorable! He's tall with golden fur and a long bushy tail. I think he likes me, he's a lot younger. But you know what they say about us Cougars... We've got it heads and tails over them young skinny pups. HURRY! Before his people take him back into the house. I won't take off, I promise. Oh come on... Do I really need this leash? How I am going to impress him, if I'm tied up to you. ALL right! NO leash. I'll be a good girl Mommy. I promise. Can I go now?

Woof... Woo hoo I'm free... Hey big boy... What's your name? *Brady.... What's yours? ....* **My name is Jayden.... but my humans call me J...Dee**...*woof... That's a nice name...* **Hey Brady ....Do you want to chase me around? .... Catch me if you can! ....Woof....** *Hold on Miss Jayden... slow down.... Where did you learn to run in circles like that...? You're pretty fast for a small breed....* **Yeah... Well you would be fast too, if your humans hit you with a stick....** *Who hits you Miss Jayden.? That big dope over there... I will bite him right now.....***NO! NO! NO! ... NOT these humans, other humans I use to live with.** *Oh... okay... because I would bite them if you ever want me to Miss Jayden...***That's very nice of you to offer Brady.... If I ever see them again I will let you know... You can bite them all you want! You see, Mommy and Daddy are my new humans... They never hit me**... *That's good Miss Jayden. My humans don't hit me either, they just yell at me when I go near the road....* **You had better stay away from the road Brady... I don't want to see**

you get hit by a car... I like you ...and *I like you to Miss Jayden...*

One of the guys at the pen told me he was hit by a car... and the car didn't even stop. They couldn't find his humans, so they put him in a cage, with a big cone on his neck and he couldn't even lick his wounds.... *Woof that sounds terrible! Why were you in the pen? What is the PEN anyway! How old are you Miss Jayden.? How long have you lived here? What is that scar on your head? When do we....?* **SLOW down! Slow Down..! You ask a lot of questions Brady.** *I'm sorry Miss Jayden! But I am excited to have a friend! Will you be my friend? Will ya? Huh? Will ya? Huh?* **Of course I will be your friend Brady! Can you stop drooling all over me now? You're getting that stuff everywhere**. *I am sorry again Miss Jayden... I don't mean to do it.*

How old are you Miss Jayden? .... **Well.... if you must know I am about 10 years old. But I am a young 10... Also ... I've never had puppies, so I still have my girlish figure...** *And it's a pretty one. I like what you do with your* *tail, curl it over your back like that.* **Brady stop! You're making me blush.** *What is the Pen? How did you get that scar? What is the?.* **Slow down big fella! You're starting to drool again. So anyway, the pen is short for dog Pen or Penitentiary for you college educated humans. And it is a BAD, bad place, with lots of small cages.** *What are cages?* **Boy you don't know much of anything do ya?** *I'm sorry Miss Jayden.... I'm only 1 years old....,* **(this is gonna be more of a challenge than I thought. Oh well... so he isn't too bright.... at least he has his charm and good looks)** *Miss Jayden, You're so smart, Can you teach me more? Can Ya? Can ya?*

    Ok ...Listen up Lance. Because this could save your life someday. *Okay Miss Jayden let me sit down so I can stare into your beautiful eyes......* **(Ohhh my God where have you been all my life... a girl could get her heart broken with this charmer)... Easy does it Fabio! We just met... so as I was saying. The pen can be a bad, bad place.**

Humans bring dogs there when they have been bad. Or when they just get sick of taking care of us.

The pen guards are really nice. They try to find us new homes... But when they can't, you're stuck in the cage all day. Nice humans come at night to take you for a walk. They try really hard to find new homes for us, but it seems like the cute little puppies get taken home first. People seem to think you can't teach an old dog new tricks. But it's actually the opposite....

We know not to chew slippers and shoes.... *Oh we aren't.... is that why my Daddy was mad at me? I didn't know... I'm only 1 years old....* Well you better wise up. A pretty boy like you wouldn't last in the pen. There are some tough dogs in the pen. Rottie's, Pits...Dobie's. *OK Miss Jayden, I wouldn't chew on Daddy's slippers anymore, so what can I chew? ....* Bones and furry stuffed toys, for some strange reason humans think we like chewing on animal bones. I keep telling my humans, I like the meat on the bone.... but Daddy eats all the meat and I just get the bone... but if you CHEW , CHEW & CHEW some more, there's a small amount of soft meat in the middle? .... *Boy Miss Jayden, how did you get so smart?* **When I was in the pen, I listened to all of the story's that got told, while hanging around the hydrant,** *Please tell me a story Miss Jayden... Huh! Huh! Please.* **Alright, alright! Stop slobbering all over the place...** *Okay! Now tell me a story... please! Please!*

Brady you act like you've never been with a girl before... *I've never been with anybody before. You're my first dog friend. I saw a cat once, but he scratched my nose. Then my Mommy yelled at him and I never saw him again. My nose hurt really bad and I was afraid because....* **Hey! Chatter BOX! Do you want me to tell my story or not?** *Yes Miss Jayden... Sorry Miss Jayden...* **Okay, but let's get some water to wash up with. You look a little silly with all that drool on your face. And enough of the {Miss Jayden crap.}. You're making me feel so old! Call me Jayden or JJ...I'm only 70. That's 10 in human years. I should live to be well over**

100.... That's because I am I small breed ... We live longer than large breed dogs... *But the drool doesn't bother me... Miss Jayden.* {This charmer's got the looks ...but he's about as bright as a 20 watt light bulb}....

Really... You can't feel that...Yuk. Let's get that slime of your face. Your humans are going to think you have rabies... *What are rabies Miss Jayden?* Come on ya big slug, let's wash the slime off your face first... We can go to your house, I don't want that sludge in my water bowl. *O.k. Miss Jayden... follow me. I have a bowl outside on the back porch...Here we are...*

Okay now Brady, stick your snout deep in the water bowl... Now shake off all that drool...blub blubbl blub... *O.K. Miss Jayden... How does that look.* That looks better! Now I can talk to you, without laughing. *You're funny Miss Jayden. I like you.* Okay, so you want to make your humans happy. Chase the ball and bring it back when they throw it. Don't ask me why, but they like to play ball a lot. But don't worry, they get tired rather quickly. With all your drool they won't want to pick up the ball once you bring it back anyway...And they like to go for long walks. So pretend you want to go to... jump up and down, stuff like that*... Oh... OK Miss Jayden.* **And don't beg for food. There is always somebody that's willing to give you food. Just sit there and look pretty. My humans have an ole guy who keeps food in his pockets for me...** *What else Miss Jayden? ... Tell me more, tell me more, this is fun...* **Easy, ya big Moose! You're starting to drool all over me again.** *Sorry Miss Jayden....*

   O.K Brady. That's enough for now... I will tell you about the Pen later.... it's getting dark out and I don't want to scare you... *Woof! Please tell me more! I won't cry or get scared...* **Well Ok, Just one more thing. Don't even think about driving the car by yourself... I keep asking and asking but they won't let me! They do let me stick my head out of the window, but with all your drool... You may have to wash the car when you get back....**

And don't forget to do your business before you get in the car. Because you never know how long you will be locked in there. You have got that slime thing going on, so you may not get thirsty. But I get really thirsty sticking my head out the window... *Thanks Miss Jayden, thank you so much... I'm going to do everything you said, you are so smart...* Alright... Alright... Don't get all wishy washy on me...I am going to take a nap... I need my beauty rest. Come back out tomorrow, I will teach you more. *Okay! Bye Miss Jayden .I can't wait to see you again...* Yeah, Yeah! Just make sure you wash all the slime of your face before you come out tomorrow. Maybe you should start carrying a hankie or better yet, a drool bucket... *Awww Miss Jayden ...It's not that bad ....Is it?* I'm just pulling your tail Brady... Ha ha....Goodbye for now Brady... *Goodbye Miss Jayden...*

Ya gotta love that big Oaf... Isn't that always the case? ...All beauty and no brains... Typical man.... at least he is nice to me... not like those pedigree boys in the Pen, always stealing my food, hiding my bones and calling me bad names, like mixed breed. They are such

Bullies... And NOBODY likes getting bullied... It's not my fault I don't know my Daddy's breed. My Mommy was a Chow and Daddy might have been a golden retriever... I have got a few brothers and sister... I haven't seen any of them since my first humans took me away... I wish I could see them again...But I don't know where to start looking...

Woof ... Mommy is calling me, coming Mommy. Here I am. I was just talking to Brady. He's the handsome boy that just moved in next door... NO... he is not my boyfriend Mommy. Stop it, you're making me blush... Can I take a nap before supper? I am tired from playing with Brady, he is so young and full of energy OK... wake me up for supper please, Thanks Mommy...

I must have slept right through supper... Aww... my favorite too. I can smell it in the trash. Mommy's roast beef, potatoes, and gravy, woof... I better not mess with the trash... I did that at my bad human's house and I got a boot right in the tail. I couldn't sit down for a week. I don't think Daddy would do that to me, but I'm not going to take any chances... Hey, maybe I could get Brady to dig it out of the trash. He's just dumb enough to do it... nah I couldn't do that to the loveable lug... But Mommy's roast beef just melts in your mouth... Maybe I'll get the bone before Daddy chews all the meat off of it. Well I had better get back to work. I thought I heard a noise out back. I hope it's not that stink bomb again... I thought they would never let me back in the house the way I smelled. I had better tell my new B F F about the smelly cat... he already drools all over himself... he doesn't need a bad smell to go along with it...

Woof! ...Stop right there...Or I'll Bite your ...OH...Sorry Daddy. You Startled me. I was day dreaming about Mommy's roast beef. Oh hey...Before you throw that in the trash, do you think I could have the scraps in there? ... Oh NO...Stop Don't throw that on top of it....Aww Yuk...Now you've got saw dust and wood chips all over it... I don't think even the squirrels

would eat it now, and they eat anything... Hey!
Slick...I'm talking to you. When are you going to
learn to speak dog? Daddy, don't you know this
is my (I love roast beef face...) I know that I slept
through supper, but it's not my fault! Brady had
me running around in circles chasing my tail. I
haven't done that in a long time. I think since you
first rescued me from the pen. Remember
Daddy? I was spinning around and around, then
I slipped and fell over, we laughed so hard, you
shot soda out your nose. Remember?
Yah...Those were the Days...

    It's hard to believe we've been together for
this long. Seems like yesterday we were cruising
home in Mommy's convertible, boy how time
flies, for a dog anyway. For you it's only been 6
years but, for me it's been 42... That makes me
70 years old... Woof... The days go by so quickly
when you get treated like a queen ... not like my
younger days when I sat in the backyard all by
myself. I was so lonely. Time seemed to stand

still... Well enough of this depressing talk... where was I? Oh yeah... Mommy's roast beef. Sooo Daddy... Do you think we can go in that big white food box and get the bone from Mommy's roast beef...? Only this time, could you leave a little meat on it for me... You have already eaten your share! Besides if you were a dog your belly would be dragging on the ground like that hound dog down the street... Oopsie... Did that come out loud? Talk like that isn't going to get me a bone. Luckily, Daddy's dog whispering skills are on the first grade level....

Mommy knows what I'm thinking all the time. Well, at least she thinks she does... like when she takes me on a long, long walk... Sometimes just a short walk to Grandma's house is just right.... Hey Daddy you going back in? Wait for me! Maybe I'll save that bone for tomorrow, Daddy.... It's getting kind of late. You can go sit with Mommy and watch the noisy squawk box in the parlor... I'm going to sleep... I mean, Ahh, I'm going to check the house for burglars and thieves. No worries Daddy! I'm on the job! Say good night to Mommy for me. Goodnight Daddy.....

Good morning everybody! Rise and shine! Somebody has to let me out, come on.... Let's go! Hurry! I can't hold it much longer... I've got some serious business to take care of ...

HURRY ... HURRY... I'll be at the door.... Awww... Thanks Daddy... I don't think I could've held it any longer, that was a close one. Hey Daddy where we going today? Can we go in the truck? Can we? Huh? Can we? .... Awww come on... Are you and Mommy gonna ride that two wheeled noise maker again? When are you going to let me try it? Hey! What's that box where Mommy usually sits? ...Whoa! ... HEY! Put me down! Wait just one minute! I was just kidding! Daddy! Hey! Get me off this crazy thing! Have you gone nuts or something? Mommy help! Daddy's gone crazy! ....Oh no! He has lost his mind... Hey take those funny goggles off my eyes!

OH NO.... Mommy! Help... Here we go... oh my god! I'm scared!

BBBBbrrrr oooooooom mmm Brroo oommm.... Hey this isn't so bad, not bad at all. As a matter of fact, It's kind of fun. I've got the wind in my fur, the sun shining on me. Hey look Daddy, a squirrel! Get him, yeah! Haaa! ...Holy cow.... This is awesome! Look another squirrel, get HIM! Geez ! This thing is fast! Circle around Daddy, I think we can get them on the way back. Woof ... Daddy let's go to the park... There's always a lot of squirrels there. Awww... Don't go back home. Hey there is Mommy ... I think she's taking my picture.... Turn this thing around, I want her to get my good side... Awww... Don't stop Daddy! I was just getting the hang of this thing... I can't wait to tell Brady... aww... Don't take me off! WELL... Okay, I guess Mommy want a turn... You two hurry back... I'll be here, keeping an eye on things... Hold on tight Mommy! Daddy goes really fast... Bye ... Have fun!

I need a drink of water! (Cough, cough) I think I swallowed a bug or two... But that's okay... that was the most fun I've ever had my life... Daddy was laughing too, when I started talking to him using my throaty people voice. I think that's the first time I've ever talk to Daddy and made him laugh, really hard ... I was whispering in his ear how much fun it was. I think he knows, cuz I have never talked like that to a human before. I think he finally understands me. Well, I could sure use a nap. All that excitement takes a lot out of ya... I had better dig a hole to lay in first. It is getting awfully hot out here...Nice day for an afternoon snooze...

Hey! It's getting dark out here. I hope they didn't forget me, it's been a long time since I had to sleep outside all by myself... bbrrooooommm... broooommmmm... I hear them coming... Hey Mommy ... Hey Daddy! Where did you go? I was getting worried... Did you catch any squirrels? I didn't think so, that thing is too noisy, they hear you coming a mile away. Hey Mommy. Let's go for a little walk. Oh geez. Wait. What's in the bag? Sniff,sniff, Ohh Food... OK... Maybe we can eat first! Then we can go for a walk. I was hoping to see Brady, so I could tell him about my ride on the noise maker. So what's in the bag? Awww...! Burgers and fries! Yummy... Just like the day we met, remember. Boy these are really good. Oh some chicken too! Yeah, that's what I'm talking about. Hey Mommy, maybe we can go for a walk tomorrow, I'm feeling kinda full. I am kind of sleepy now too... okay I'll be in my chair in the window...

Good morning Mommy. Good morning Daddy. I'm going over to Mr. Perry's house. He's the nice guy that lives behind us. I'm going to work security for his wife, while he is sick. I've got the feeling he doesn't have much longer to live. I'll be close by. Just call me if you need me....

"Ring"... "Ring", "ring", "ring"... Hello... This is Mrs. Perry, Your neighbor right behind you. Your dog is really sweet and she's oh so very nice. But she has been sitting on my porch all day. And she keeps chasing away the mailman and the paper boy. I was wondering if you could come and get her. You see my husband has been really sick. And I know he loved talking with her, when she's in the back yard. He would give her treats, throw her the ball, he would go out to see her almost every day. She is really a sweet dog, and I like her too. But I need my newspaper and my mail. I don't know why she feels that I need protection. Could you come and get her please... Thank you...

I'm coming Mommy! Here I am. What do you mean I can't go over there anymore? I was just trying to be a good dog. You see I got this feeling Mr. Perry is sick and he needs my help. So I secured the property. Nobody was going to get by me. Okay Mommy. I'm Sorry. I won't leave the yard. I just got a feeling we won't be seeing Mr. Perry in his backyard anymore. And I wanted to go say goodbye. He was always so nice to me. He would give me food and ham bones. And he would talk to me all the time... He was my friend, and I don't have many good friends like him. Well Now I feel like he's not going to be there for me anymore. I don't know how I do it? It's just, some dogs can feel it. No special tricks... just like I know when Daddy doesn't feel good. I just sense it. It's like I feel his thoughts in my bones, and I know Mr. Perry is not going to make it. I didn't tell Mrs. Perry. She has enough to worry about. She's a nice lady too... OK Mommy ... I'm sorry. I didn't mean to worry you. I hope I am wrong and Mr. Perry is ok...

My, it's getting cold out again... It feels cold, like when the white stuff falls from the sky. I must say, time sure is flying by. Pretty soon everybody will come over to eat turkey and drink, and then eat some more. Then they all sit around the flashy box on the wall and yell and scream at it... These humans are sure strange creatures. But I don't know what I'd do without them...

Mommy, Daddy, can I go out. I see Brady outside. Can I? Can I, come on please? I don't need a leash.

Thanks Daddy. You can come too. Hey Brady! Hey Brady! Where have you been*? Hi Miss Jayden. Where have you been Miss Jayden? I haven't seen you all summer...* **My humans have been keeping me busy most every day... We went to the beach and stayed in a little house on the water, and we went swimming everyday...** *My human kept me busy too. We go to this big farm and they have horses and I get to run around and play.*

I don't have to worry about cars on the farm either... I got to play with the Pigs and the goats...I had so much fun... It sounds like you had FUN too...

Yah good buddy. I did...You're getting smarter every day! You still got that drooling thing going on tho...huh*... Sorry Miss Jayden, I think it's cuz I'm a large breed. That's what the vet told my Daddy. I only do it when I'm happy and I'm always happy when I see you Miss Jayden.* **{Boy he is getting good at the smooth talk or is it smooth with the good talking} Oh, Brady! You're so nice to me...**

Let's play. Catch me if you can. *Woof... okay... Hey... slow down! You're so fast Miss Jayden....***Oh Yah ... That was fun... I can't run like I used to though**... *I'm a little tired too Miss Jayden...* **Let's go get some water. You got some of that drool on your face.** *Sorry Miss Jayden.* **That's okay Brady... Just a little bit of slime is kind of cute!**

   Hey Brady did I tell you I can ride a motorcycle? *What's a motorcycle?* **It's that loud thing Mommy and Daddy fly around on. I sit behind Daddy and we go really fast, and we chase squirrels... And the sun is shining on your face and the wind blows thru your fur, it's just a great feeling...** *Do you think I can ride a motorcycle Miss Jayden?* **I'm not sure Brady you're kind of heavy and with those big broad shoulders of yours, you may not fit in the Box Daddy made.** *That's okay Miss Jayden. As long as you tell me stories. I'm happy.* **You're so sweet Brady. I'm glad I have you to talk to.** *I'm. The lucky one Miss Jayden.*

   Oh no ...My dad is calling me. But I don't want to go. *You better go Miss Jayden. You don't want to get in* *trouble... you don't want to make him mad...* **I don't worry about getting hit anymore. I know Daddy would never hurt me.** *That's* good *Miss Jayden. I worry about you. My humans never hurt me.* **Uht oh, here he comes. I should go. Bye Brady. I love you**... *Good bye Miss Jayden... What does love mean?* **I'll tell you next time. I gotta go... {He's getting older, but not much smarter. Luckily, he's one handsome Labrador}...**

Here I am Daddy. I was just talking to Brady. No he's not my boyfriend. I like him a lot. But... But... oh well, maybe he is my boyfriend. But don't tell him that. He will start drooling all over the place... Is it bed time already Daddy? I was having so much fun with Brady, I lost track of time....Ok good night Daddy...I'll be in my chair, say good night to Mommy for me.

Mommy ... Daddy ...Help! I can't stop coughing... HELP! {Cough} {Cough!} {Cough} There you are... {Cough} {Cough} I don't know

what's happening! [Cough} {Cough} I can't breathe Mommy {cough} rub my throat.... Mommy ... Please! Please! I think we need to go to the emergency Vet, you know the one I don't like. But he is the only Vet open this late at night. Daddy can you carry me? I'm really scared. Please hurry! Can you put me in the back seat with Mommy? Woof. Let's go Buckle up Mommy. Ok Daddy, she is locked in....Let's Roll ....

WOOF... Hold on Mommy! I never saw Daddy drive so fast. Go! Daddy go! Drive it like you stole it Daddy! No need to stop at the red lights! Go... go! .... Boy, Daddy sure is a good driver. Don't worry Mommy ... I'll be okay... You can relax... Stop crying, you don't want to make Daddy nervous.... Hey Stupid.! Watch out! Sick dog coming through! ... Woof...That was a close call. Keep going Daddy, don't stop now...

Woof... That was fast! We are here already. Can you carry me in? Please Daddy, I'm too weak to stand on my own...

HI nice lady in blue! Are you the doctor? Cough! Cough. I can't catch my breath and I keep coughing. Can you help me? Ok, thanks... Can Mommy and Daddy come in with me? I am scared. Hey! Where are you taking me? Oh no, small cages! I know what that means...Woof...Oh Another nice lady in blue. Hey, what are you doing? Don't be shaving my paw. That's gonna look funny, well okay! I'll even let you stick me with that needle, but only if it makes me feel better... Ouch! That hurts! That had better stop me from coughing! What now? Some pills? Ohh...Just give it to me! You don't have to put in a biscuit. I'm not a gullible little puppy! I know all of those human tricks... Woof... What next? Oh No! Not the cage! I freak out in cages! Well, at least I can see Daddy. He's been peeking in thru the small window on the door.

What's this! Air is blowing in my face. Well that feels good. I can breathe easier already, and my chest doesn't hurt much anymore. I'm feeling a little funny tho! Kind of woozy... Boy, what was in that shot? This feels kinda good. I kinda feel like that boozer with the lamp shade on his head...

Woof. Hey look. There is Mommy and Daddy. Yo yo... yo... Whaz up Daddy-o.? Ha-ha sorry Mommy .... I'm feeling a little goofy.... Daddy you better carry me. I don't know what was in that shot but I feel like I can fly... Wooohff ... Hey did I just bark? I think I did. I think I need to lay down, before I fall down! This feels freaky. Wake me up when we get home, will you please Mommy?

Hey Mommy ... You got that salt water coming from your eyes again. Don't worry Mommy! I'll be okay! Oh no, not you too Daddy! Look, I'm OK...Woof... Well I can't stand up now, but I'm really okay! I just need to take a nap. You just watch where you're going Daddy. I'm too tired to drive, and I'm feeling kinda woozy... You don't have to drive so fast now, Daddy...I don't know what is worse? Having a heart attack from being old or having one from Daddy's driving! I think we broke a land speed record.

Don't worry…I'm okay Mommy … Kiss… Kiss… I just need to rest… Kiss, Kiss, I just have to take it easy. No more long walks. I can still go for walks Mommy. I just can't go as far as we use to. I might not be that good of a watchdog either. My eyes are a little blurry and I can't hear everything either. You still love me? Don't you Mommy? Kiss…Kiss… Sorry Mommy. Don't look so sad, I wouldn't let anybody hurt you! I can still bark! Woof …And show my teeth! Grrr… That will scare burglars & thieves. Wont it? I just need some sleep. It been a long night. Can I sleep on your lap Mommy? I am feeling a little woozy still…

Oh wow, we're home already! I must have dozed off. I'm still a little dopy. How did I get in the house? OH. Daddy must have carried me. Thanks Daddy! What's going on now? You don't have to sleep on the floor with me. Mommy! Daddy! I'm okay! Well if you insist. This is kind of cozy. Goodnight Mommy ... Goodnight Daddy. I love you. Thanks for taking care of me. Don't tell Brady about my heart problem. I don't want him to worry about me. I'll be okay. Besides... He will only get all mushy and drool all over me...And I don't feel like getting a bath ...and then needing a bath. Good Night. I love you. Thank you for taking care of me. You are the best parents a dog could have...

Alright..! Mommy and Daddy are having a lot of people over to eat, drink and sit around the fire pit in the backyard. Daddy always lets me run free. And Mommy plays hide and seek with me. Sometimes I go near the road, and she yells at me... but I run over and hide behind Daddy, he knows I won't run away. Sometimes they warm up tasty white gooey gobs on a stick, over the fire. They are really Ooey and gooey and get stuck to the roof of my mouth. I have to lick and lick and lick, to get if off. I must look funny because everybody laughs at me, but I don't care. They taste so good! Sometimes I get a tasty crackers to go with it.

The humans have chocolate with theirs but I can't have chocolate because I get sick. One time I ate a piece of chocolate off the ground, and I got sick so bad, I pooped all over myself. It went everywhere! Then Daddy gave me a bath, after he cleaned up my chair. It was horrible! I'll never do that again! Woof... Hey Mommy is not looking. I think I'll go for a little stroll over to Brady's house. ...

Woof, woof... Hey Brady can you come out and play? I guess you must be sleeping, it is kind of late .Maybe I'll go for a stroll around the neighborhood. Hey, what's that across the street? I think I'll go check it out while Mommy's not looking. Woof... Whatever it is, it's gone now. It was probably that stink bomb of a cat with the white tail again. Oh no! Here comes Mommy!

And she doesn't look happy! I'd better run and hide.

Screeeeech....Bang... Help! Help! I've been hit by a car. I can't move my leg, oh... Wow it hurts...Mommy ... It hurts so badly. I can't move my leg. Ouch! It hurts Mommy, it hurts. Woof... Here is the lady that was driving the car. Don't yell at her Mommy! It's not her fault! I ran right out in front of her. Don't yell at me either. Not now at least. Mommy, I'm in a lot of pain! Ouch, ouch ... Here comes Daddy, and BOY does he look mad! Don't yell at me Daddy, Please! Daddy can you carry me? My back leg hurts really, really bad. Thanks Daddy... Ouch, ouch, ouch! Okay, okay. Put me down... let me see if I can put some weight on it. Ouch, I better hold it up off the ground. Oh no! I think I'm in trouble! It's not Mommies fault Daddy... She tried to grab me and I ran. Oh wow! I think it's broken. If I was just a little faster, the car would have missed me. Ouch! Ouch! I hate to say this but I may have to go back to the vet. Can you carry me to the car Daddy? Thank you... You're my hero...

Okay... I will sit in the back seat with Mommy. Can I lean on you, Mommy? I'm sorry Mommy. I thought you were mad at me so I ran. I didn't see the car coming. I'm not as fast as I used to be. I can't see very well either...Don't hit any bumps Daddy! And Daddy, Please don't drive so fast, I'll be okay. One of the girls in the pen got hit by a car and she was just fine. Oh! We're here already, boy Daddy drives fast... Ouch! Ouch! ... I thought I could walk on it... Daddy you'd better carry me...

Hi nice lady in blue. It's me again. This time, I got struck by a car and my leg hurts really bad. Can you help me again...OK...Up we go. Listen Sweetie. I will take the pills, you don't have to hide it in the food. If it helps my leg feel better. I will eat almost anything...woo hooo, that pill works really fast, I feel real sleepy already.... okay goodnight...

Hey. What happened? How come my back legs are tied together? When I was sleeping I thought I heard the lady say my leg popped out of the socket. Whatever that means. Well at least it's not broken. That's good! Hey, there's Mommy & Daddy ... Daddy, help me get the tape off my legs I can't walk... What's with this cone on my head? Come on Daddy, pick me up, let's get out of here... I'm still a little woozy, I think you had better drive. I'll sit with Mommy in the backseat. Mommy can you get this cone of my head, I think I'm picking up HBO or something. Alright I'll just sit and relax... but when I get home I'm chewing this thing off...

Okay Daddy, I think we're home now. Hey! There's Brady...Hey Brady... *HI Miss Jayden. Where have you been? I have been worried about you. What is that thing on your head? And why are your legs tied together?* Hey Sexy...You are SO handsome... I love you... *Miss Jayden. Why are you slurring your words? Are you drunk?* No silly, I went to close to the road and got hit by a car! I had to go to the vets. He put this cone on my head and gave me a pill and I'm still a little woozy.... Can we talk later Brady? I need to go lie down and sleep this off.....

Ok Daddy... You can carry me in now....Good bye Brady...Stay away from the road...*Good Bye Miss Jayden. I'll be right here if you need me...*Ok lover boy...I will always Love....Hey wait Daddy! I wasn't done talking with my boyfriend... Ouch ...That's starting to hurt again. Can I have another pill Daddy? Thanks Daddy...You take such good care of me... I think I'll sleep on the floor so I don't fall out of my chair. These pills are strong.... They're making me hungry.... Woof....My this is some crazy stuff. I can't even get up.

WHY am I sooo hungry! Yo Yo daddio... Can you get me a snack? Daddy O, yo I got the munchies. Ouch hey, what was that? Ohh... that was me. Wow... this is some crazy stuff. I had better skip the chow and go to sleep. I'm feeling kind of kooky. Well at least my leg doesn't hurt anymore. Goodnight Daddy, goodnight Mommy. Thanks for taking such good care of me. Kiss. Lick. Kiss...

Thanks Mommy ... I thought you were never going to take that cone off my head...LOOK... Mommy! Mommy! There is Brady, out in the backyard. Can I go out ...Can I...? Can I.... Okay I'll go out on the leash. Anything! Just let me out of this house. YO... Brady. I miss you so much Brady. *Go easy Miss Jayden your legs are still taped together.* **I know. I know. Brady will you help me chew it off...** *Oh NO. I can't do that Miss Jayden. I will get in trouble.* **Don't be such a Nancy pants. Do it when she is not looking!** *Sorry... BUT.... I can't do that Miss Jayden. Its helping you get better...* **BUT, I am better. I keep jumping on the couch to show them I am back to normal, BUT they don't Listen....** *You had better leave it on Miss Jayden. Humans know what's best for us...* **Well O.K. Brady...I will leave it on...**

SAY...since when did you get so smart. Seems like yesterday you had drool all over your face. And you were afraid of your own shadow. How old are you now Brady? *I'm seven years old now Miss Jayden.* Yeah ...Life sure has been good to us, eyh Brady....*It sure has Miss Jayden....*It's nice you got that drooling thing under control....*Your funny Miss Jayden...*Speaking of funny...remember jamming your head in the water bowl to wash all that junk off your face...Haaa haaaa...*Quit pulling my leg Miss Jayden...*Yah, I am just messing with ya good buddy. Hey, I think your humans are calling you Brady. *Yup...I have to go now Miss Jayden...You take care of that leg now...Good Bye Miss Jayden...*BYE Brady...I love that big beluga. I can't tell him that tho. He will start drooling all over me again...Woof ...Hey Mommy, I need to go lay down. Can you carry me in? You were right, my leg isn't back to normal yet.

It's starting to get cold again. Feels good to be back to my old self. I thought they were never going to take the tape off my legs. I have started taking Mommy for walks again. We don't go as far as we used to. I've been getting tired a lot lately. I hope I am NOT coming down with something. I had all my shots this spring. Or was that last spring? I just remember they hurt. And for some strange reason they want some of my poop in one of those little pink bags. I still haven't figured out what they do with my Pooh??? Who knows? But if that's what they want, I seem to have a never ending supply. I think I may have to go to the doctors, before this cough gets much worse. Mommy rubs my Throat and it seems to feel better, but only for a little while. Let's see what Mommy says next time it happens ... It always seems to happen during the night.

Cough. Cough. Mommy! Mommy! Cough. Cough. Mommy. I can't breathe. And my chest hurts. Please Mommy. I think we need to go to the doctor again. Cough. Cough. I'm afraid! Mommy! I have to stick my head up in the air like this just to breathe. Hurry! Wake up Daddy. Cough. Cough.... He'll know what to do. Cough Hurry! Cough. There he is Mommy. We have to go to the vets Daddy. Will you carry me? Let's Go, NOW Daddy! Just hurry! Cough. Cough. Thanks Mommy, rub my throat. Cough. I guess we gotta sit in the back seat together Mommy.

Woof. Hold on Mommy. Daddy's really flying now. Hey look out buddy. Daddy's got the right of way. Sick dog coming through.... WOOF.... lookout Bustah ! Coming through... Holy cow, I think we just went up on two wheels. Slow down Daddy. You're going to kill us. I can breathe a little easier now Daddy... Cough. Cough. Boy! Were we moving? We were lucky we didn't see any policemen Daddy. I hope they would understand. After all, it's a matter of life and death! My life! And my death! Nice driving Daddy. Okay, here we go. I'll be alright Mommy. Don't cry Mommy. Cough. I'll be ok. All of the walks you took me on made me strong!

Oh. Hi lady in blue. It's me again.... Are you the nice woman who took care of me last time? Sniff, Sniff... Nope that wasn't you. Not enough cheap perfume. Woof, Woof, Oh hi Doc... It's me again....Woof. Hey that things cold... Yeah doc, it hurts right where you put that cold thing... It's kind of hard to breathe too. Cough... Cough... Hey Doc. Where you going with that big needle? Well okay, if it makes me feel better... Hey wait a minute. You're taking stuff out of me... And now you're squirting more stuff into me. I think this is when I need to close my eyes... Woof... Where we going now? Oh no.... Not one of those cages. I HATE CAGEs... HELP! ...

Get me out of here. I can't stand being in cages. Help! Get me out of here... What kind of cage is this? It's so tiny... And it has cool air blowing in my face. This feels weird. Well I can breathe easier. But now I'm freaking out because I'm in a tiny cage. Get me out of here. Can't you see that I'm freaking out? How long are you going to keep me in here? Get me out of here. My chest feels OK. Get me out of here. This is great, now they're going to think I'm crazy too. Get me out! Get me out of here...NOW!!!

Woof. There's Mommy and Daddy. I'm so happy to see you... I feel like I've been in here forever. Get me out of this sardine can. I can't stand being cooped up. Don't talk to them Daddy! They're the ones that put me in here... Wow...Daddy looks mad. And he's crying too. Come on please Daddy. Please Mommy ... Oohh thank you, thank you. Kiss, Kiss, Kiss. Mommy, Daddy, I am feeling much better. Put me up on the table over there, so we can talk. Kiss, Kiss. I love you too Daddy. I love you too Mommy. I am fine. The shots they gave me are working! I just get freaked out when I'm in a cage. Let's get out of here. Please. Please. Kiss, Kiss ... OH come on! .....Quit all the blubbering and let's go... We can talk on the way home... LET'S GO... Before they change their minds! ... WOOF...

Thanks for getting me out of that weird cage Daddy. I'm Sorry, but I could get never get used to being in a cage again. Too many bad memories. Hey, we gotta wait for Mommy. Oh... Here she is. Hold me close Mommy. I'm still a little wacked out from being in that tiny cage. Okay. I'm ready! Let's get going. We don't have to go so fast on the way home Daddy. It's dark out still. We got the whole road to ourselves. You still seem mad Daddy. What did the doctor say to get you so upset? I heard him say you should put me down. What does that mean? You were not even holding me up. I was in the cage. Mommy let's not go there anymore. I like that nice Doctor, over near our house. I'm going to sleep on the ride home, if it's OK with you Mommy? ... It's been a rough week...

Wow... We are home already. I can walk by myself Daddy. Well maybe NOT...OK...You can carry me in the house. What are you guys doing? Awww...You're gonna sleep on the floor with me again. Isn't this nice. One big happy family. HEY! I said HAPPY! You two aren't gonna Blubber all night, are ya? Because I need some beauty sleep! I thought I wasn't gonna make it to my OWN 16th birthday. We are having a big party, aren't we? Ok...let's get some sleep. Good night Daddy. Good night Mommy. I'm sorry I woke you up so late at night. ...Kiss, Kiss... I love you too...

Daddy sure makes a lot of NOISE when he sleeps...How can Mommy stand it? I'm gonna sneak out to the porch and sleep...Good night ...

Hey, Good morning Daddy...Whatch ya doing? Sneaking a smoke? You shouldn't be doing that Daddy. It's bad for you. I hear Mommy yelling at you all the time...and I don't like the smell either. I'm going to tell Mommy ... Woof... There you are Mommy. Daddy was having a smoke. Yell at him. Before he gets away! Where is he going? Let me go find out. Hey Daddy, are we going for a ride in the truck? Oh No. Mommy's coming too. I knew this was coming. Okay, let's get this over with. Just don't put me in any cages.

I'm only going because my chest hurts a little still.

Alright... Here we are. I like coming to this vet. They haven't put me in ANY cages yet. And I love the smell of this room. It smells like a box of puppies. It brings back so many memories of my brothers and sisters. Oh Hi Doc. Okay. I'm ready for you...Go ahead, put that the cold thing on my chest. Yelp... It hurts right there. And a little over to the left. Yup. No pain over there. Woohoo... that kind of tickles. Okay. Is that it? I can get down now. Yippee!

Boy that was easy. Okay let's go Daddy. Mommy you get me some pills, I'll be outside with Daddy... Woof... That was quick "n" Easy. OK Daddy. So if I take my 3 pills every day, I will be okay? Will I Daddy? Oh Daddy! Don't start crying again. I'll be okay. It's just three little pills a day. I know I'm getting slower, and I can't jump into the truck like I used too. But you're getting older too Daddy. You don't rollerblade with me to the park anymore. And I hear you moan and groan when you wake up in the morning. I know I'm older now, but I can still protect you and Mommy from burglars. My bark is still scary, listen to this... Woof.... I can growl and show my teeth See, look Grrr.... Hey don't laugh at me! ...Woof... Here's Mommy, jump in the truck mommy, let's go home.

Ohhhh... Don't cry Mommy, please. These pills make me feel better. I'll be okay. This has been one bad month, I tell ya... I think we all need to take a nap. Can I go sleep in my bed on the porch when we get home? It's cooler on the porch. You two like it way to hot in the house. You two forget, I wear a fur coat, Everyday!

Woof... Time sure is flying by. I celebrated my 16th birthday last month. Mommy gave me a ham bone with lots of meat on it. I wanted to share it with my boyfriend Brady. But he hasn't been coming outside much. He hasn't been feeling good himself. He is getting a little grey hair on the side of his nose and some around the eyes. But he is still my gorgeous Boy Toy.

My little heart goes pitter patter every time I see him! Sometimes I get all silly like a little school girl. And I chase my tail and run around in circles. He likes when I do that. He is my true love. The kind where you know what he thinks, and he knows what you think. You have the same family values, and you would protect that family with your life. No matter what! My family is the most important thing to me. I often think about the other dogs I met during my stay at the Pen. I wonder how their lives turned out. Did they find a nice family to adopt them? And I often wonder how long they had to stay in those horrible cages?

Let me tell you about this Beautiful girl I met in the Pen. Her name was Cyrus. I think she was a Greyhound super model. Because this girl was tall, thin, an Ohhh so very sexy! And talk about fast. When she escaped, nobody could catch her. Well anyway, she told us the scariest story ever! She said" she was kept in a little tiny cage most of her life. The only time they let her out was to chase a rabbit around in a big circle with a bunch of other Greyhounds... And if you were NOT at the head of the pack! They would take you to a place and this guy would stick you with a needle. You would fall asleep and you would never wake up. EVER!

Imagine being put to sleep forever. Just because you can't run fast... How come some humans are so mean and others are so nice? Cyrus said one day, a whole bunch of guys in blue uniforms busted in. They were carrying guns and wore big fancy hats. They came in and shut the place down! And Then...Get this! They brought her and hundreds of her friends to the Dog Penitentiaries all over the place... Splitting up families. Brothers and sisters sent to different homes...That's Sooo Scary... I hope somebody kind, like my Mommy and Daddy took her home, and all of her friends' got nice homes too... Because... a House is not a Home, without a Dog...

Then there was ole big boobs Beauty... Don't laugh. That's what we called her. She got that nick name because she lived in a mill that made puppies. All year long she would just make puppies. She made so many, her boobies would drag on the ground. And then one day they just took her to the pen, for no reason at all! Now Brady told me not to believe everything I heard while I was in the pen! But why would they make that stuff up.

Woof.... Wait! I hear my Mommy calling me. I think we are going for a ride in the truck. It's that time of year when they put a pretty tree in the living room and we have the whole family over. It seems like we get more people every year. The little puppy humans are getting bigger than me. And more little puppy humans are coming along. Mommy and all the lady's pass them around to each other. I got to lick the puppy human's face once. They always smell so clean and fresh. Well most of the time. For some reason, humans save their poop in a little white bag. And they make them wear the bag, so they must poop a lot! I still can't figure out why they save baby poop in little bags. Mommy still saves my poop in little pink bags. You humans are a strange bunch! But I love my whole pack of humans...Even the little ones that pull on my fur...

Last year a puppy human was pulling on my fur! So I barked at him, and nip at is hand! Well I scared the poop right out of him and made him cry! He cried the whole time his Mommy changed his poop bag. I got yelled at, by my Mommy and I had to apologize... But it was worth it, because he doesn't pull my furry anymore! Hey! It hurts! And I can't move away from them as fast as I use too...

Woof! Woof! Mommy, there's a bunch of humans at the front door. Is it that time already?

Look at all the food they are carrying! Woof.... Hey Mommy wearing glasses. Will you take me for a walk...Will ya...? Will ya....All right ...Lets go......So where have you been, I haven't taken you for a walk in years. Sorry but we can't walk as far as we used to. I haven't been myself lately. My paws can't handle the cold anymore and I lose my breath really easy. Mommy has just been going around the small block. Follow me...I'll show you the way...Did you bring some little pink bags, because I had a big Christmas feast with Mommy & Daddy'... Just come down this way and we will be home in no time...

I'm home Mommy ... Woof... What's that? It smells like ham! Can I have a piece? Oh boy! I can taste it already. What do you mean NO...Ok a treat will do for now. I'm going to take a nap. Wake me up when we're ready to eat...

Hey...Where did everybody go? I can't believe I slept right thru Christmas dinner... That walk I just went on really took my breath away, and I am STILL sleepy! Let's see what's going on outside ... Hey everybody...Wow that's a beautiful camp fire. Everybody's singing Christmas carols. Daddy must have brought out the good champagne. ....Wow! You humans sure are loud when you drink. And I am deaf in one ear and can't hear out of the other one....

Mommy, I'm going back in the house ... I'm not feeling too good....I think I'll go to sleep down stairs. When the champagne runs out, they will be back in the house, Singing & laughing. I don't feel like celebrating this year. I am just so tired lately, and my chest hurts a little. Not like when I fell out of the truck, deep inside my chest....Maybe I just need a good night's sleep...

Good morning Daddy. Let's go out. I got business to take care of...WOOF...Well look at this! Where did all this white stuff come from? It must have fallen from the sky last night.... (I wonder if Daddy will take me plowing.). I miss riding in the truck. It's getting harder to stand up in it. The seats are slippery and I've been falling over a lot. Even when Daddy seat belts me to the seat, I still bounce around a lot. Nope, no ride today I guess. Daddy, let me sniff over here. I wonder if I can make it over this stuff to go and see Brady. Wow this is deep! I gotta jump like a rabbit, just to get over it... woof....

Wow... I made it to the tree! I gotta catch my breath. Oh boy everything is getting blurry! I'm feeling light headed. Oh no... everything is getting dark. I can't seem to catch my breath. What's going on? I...I....don't know what's happening. Where am I going? I feel like I'm floating up in the air. It's like I have wings.

Woof...this is weird. Wait a minute... What's that down there? Is that Daddy? What is he doing? Is that me lying on the ground? Why is my tongue hanging out of my mouth? How come I'm not moving? Hey! Me... Get up! What am I doing? Look! Daddy's picking me up. Where is he going with me? Oh my god! Did I just poop on him? I think I did! How embarrassing. I hope he's not mad. He must be mad because he's banging on my chest, and running in the house with me.

How can I be floating up here when Daddy has me down there? This is a strange feeling. I'm seeing all sorts of colors. Red greens blues and yellows. I think it's a start of a rainbow. I can hear dogs barking... Wow, these colors are so pretty... WOOOF.... and now it's going away. Oh my. There is Daddy again. He has me on the floor and he's pushing on me. What the heck is he doing? He keeps pushing me and pushing me! I feel like I'm floating down, really fast... Lookout Daddy! I'm floating right behind you! Look out ME! ...... it's ME! I am heading right at myself.... WHAT should I do? I think I' m going to crash into myself... Look out DADDY!!!

Cough! Cough! Cough! Ok! Ok! Let me up! What the heck was that? Why was I floating around? What's was up with all the rainbow colors? Was that a bridge? Was I an angel? I'm scared Daddy! What just happened? Did I poop and pee on myself? I don't believe did that .That was gross! So, why were you pushing on Me? Woof...I'm feeling really weak. Can we go sit in the chair together? I need to rest. Will you carry me Daddy? Okay thanks. I love you daddy!

Oh my god! Mommy! Mommy! You should have seen Daddy. He swooped in and rescued me from heaven. He was amazing. He was banging on my chest, and I was floating away, and just when...WOOF Ohhh...Don't cry Daddy! I'm Ok now...lick, lick, lick...I was scared too Daddy. Please don't cry...I'm OK...

So Mommy! You should have seen Daddy go! He scooped me up and ran with me, as I was floating away to heaven. I saw Daddy jumping over the snow banks, running with me into the house ...Then I floated over the clouds and saw all these pretty colors, it was like a bridge, made from a rainbow, and there were a bunch of dogs calling my name ....then BANG! ...I was floating back down. Kinda falling from the sky. I looked down and I saw Daddy crouching over the other Me. Pushing on me. So I barked...LOOK out Daddy! And, then I went flying right thru Daddy and crashed into myself....I Know....Crazy Huh, I don't believe it myself... It all happened so fast...

Was I Daddy? Was I in angel? Was I supposed to cross over the rainbow bridge? Did you see me floating away and pull me back? Thanks Daddy! I never want to leave you and Mommy. I love you both so much. I'm sorry I made a mess of your jacket! I didn't mean it! It's like it wasn't even me. Before I knew it, I was flying like an angel. I flew all the way to heaven and somebody pushed me back...It all happened in a flash. I was Sooo Scared! Daddy... You are my whole life! I couldn't imagine being with anybody else!

First you and Mom and save me from the dog pen, and now you saved my life again. How can I ever repay you? I wish I was a better watch dog. Just like I used to be when I was young. But I am getting older now and I can't see or hear very well anymore. You're not going to bring me back to the Pen, are you? Cause I met a few old dogs in the pen. And their owners left them there because they were old and kept pooping on the rug a lot. I know you and Mommy would never do that. I'm sorry Daddy, I'm just rambling. This has been a very rough day. I'm going to sleep now. Can you keep hugging me, till I fall asleep Daddy. Thanx... It feels so good...Good night Mommy ...I love you...

Boy I feel a lot better today! ...Woof... Where is everybody? Hey Mommy. What are you doing? You got your sneakers on. Are we going for a walk? Huh? Huh. Can we? Can we? Come on. Let's go..... Alright Woohoo..... Here we go. Don't forget to bring the pink bags. I feel pretty good this morning Mommy. How come we're only going around the yard? Hey.... I can make it all the way around the block. Look I will even chase that squirrel. Woof.... Woof.... cough... cough... I guess you're right Mommy. Maybe we should take it slow. I feel tired just from chasing that squirrel a short distance, and I didn't even come close to catching him...

Hey! There's Brady... let's go see Brady... Hurry...Hurry Mommy ... Hey Brady....*Hey Miss Jayden... How come you're breathing so heavy Miss Jayden? Did you just run around the block with your Mommy?* No? I just chased a squirrel up the tree! And I almost caught him too..... *Boy Miss Jayden you still got what it takes. Sorry Miss Jayden, but I have to cut this short. We are on our way to the dog park to run around and play. I'll see you when I get back....Bye now Miss Jayden...*BYE Brady.

I didn't want to tell Brady about my heart problems. I don't want him to worry about me. You see, Brady has health problems of his own. I heard his Mommy say he is going to the vet and NOT the dog park. That's because he is still a big fraddy cat when it comes to going to the vets. His

Mommy said something about a rash, it must be those red spots around his nose. It's probably from all of that drool. Hey! I taught him how to wash it off by sticking your head in the water bowl, he just isn't too swift. Cute as a bunny but soft like butter....if ya know what I'm saying...

Boy, I'm Beat... I'm just tired ALL of the time lately. Taking those pills everyday seems to make me sleepy. I don't have any energy to chase squirrels or anything. The weather is getting warmer out and Mommy is gonna want to go for walks soon. I hope it doesn't hurt her feelings when I say NO. It's not that I don't wanna go. I don't think I can make it around the yard, never mind all the way around the block. I've been having accidents in the middle of the night too. I'm glad Mommy & Daddy understand. I haven't even been sleeping in the bedroom, I don't wanna make them mad at me, for peeing on the rug...

When I was in the pen, Ole man Magoo was brought there for peeing on the rug one too many times. We called him Magoo because he could not see, and he would walk into things. We all helped him walk around and find his way back and forth to the chow line. He did not even have to go in a cage. He could not see an open door to run away if it hit him on the nose. He was a smart dog, with some great stories...I miss him the most out of all my Pen friends.

Woof! Woof! Woof! DADDY......Help me! Daddy! I can't stop shaking....an it's getting really cold in here. Help Daddy Help. I am scared Daddy. We had better hurry to the vets...No time to wait for Mommy to get home... LET'S GO NOW ... Everything is getting dark ...Ok here we go. ...Hey... Why did you put me on the floor of the truck? I never ride down here. Ok. I'll stay here. I probably couldn't hold myself up anyway.

Drive faster Daddy...I'm feeling really weak. Are you still there Daddy? I can't hear you...Everything is getting dark again.

Daddy! DADDY!! Where am I? It's like I am floating on a cloud. Everything is so peaceful and quiet. Oh so Quiet. Like there is NO noise at all...

What's that? Hey! It's that giant rainbow again....WOOF .... This is weird! Hey? I can walk again, and I am not in any pain either. And I can hear again too. I think I hear my name being called. And it's coming from the other side of the rainbow ....

I can't believe this is happening, I didn't get a chance to say good bye to Mommy, Or to Daddy. A chance to say I LOVE YOU, one last time. I am gonna miss the way Mommy would kiss me on the head, the way she would tickle between my toes...Or how Daddy would just sit with me after a hard day's work and scratch behind my ears for hours...

But most of all ....I didn't get a chance to THANK them for saving me from a life at the PEN. For opening up their home to me and letting me be a part of their lives. For loving me and feeding me. Showing me DOGS DO NOT belong in cages. I'm gonna miss the long walks we would take by the river, so I could chase the squirrels, and all the rides in the truck, and on the back of Daddy's motorcycle. But most of all, I am gonna miss the taste of the tears they cried for me when I was sick. Because that my human friends! Is the sweetest taste in the world...

I have one last wish before I pass over this colorful bridge. I wish Mommy & Daddy would push aside the pain and heartache I have inflicted upon them... and fill their home and their hearts with another rescue dog from the pen. In exchange, that dog will protect you, Love you, and fill the emptiness that I have left in their home, in their hearts and in their lives... ALL MY LOVE   Jayden xx oo xx

Woof... What is this place? Woof! Look at that handsome Samoyed. My! That's a silky

white coat, with a curling, fuzzy tail, just like mine. Oh no! He's coming to talk to me. What do I say? *Hello Jayden! We have been waiting for you!* **How do you know my name? Sniff! Sniff! ... Hey! I've smelled you before. At my house.** *That's right my name is Edgar. Your Daddy rescued me. 30 years ago. That's 210 in dog years. But that's beside the point.*

Listen to me. We have to work fast. Cuz it's a long trip back. And you need to do this and do it NOW... We only have a few days that you can get thru to them, and communicate your feelings to them. The remaining part of your journey you will be invisible to them. You will always have a place in their heart and thoughts, but they will not be able to see you or hear you. They will just be able feel your thoughts, like they've done for all of these years...

Ok Edgar! Don't just stand there posing for animal crackers. Let's go! ... Woof... *Jayden come this way. We can take the dragonfly.* **DRAGONFLY! What the?** *Don't ask a lot of questions. Just jump in.* **Alright. Don't get testy. I'm jumping! I'm jumping. Let's Do this!** *So*

*Jayden. Your one of the lucky ones, you must have connections up here, because you're long overdue. .***So that was you on the Rainbow Bridge...Yeah! I remember seeing the light.... The next thing I know, I'm in Daddy's arms. And he is banging on my chest!** *Yeah, Daddy is a fighter! He didn't want to let you go. I guess the big guy upstairs must have been watching and felt sorry. But for all of his efforts, he granted you a six-month reprieve.* **Wow. THAT was nice. 12 months would have been better.**

Woof ...I hear ya there Jayden. Daddy saved my life completely! I was scheduled to get hit by a car. And Daddy adopted me, you see my dog tag there hanging off the rear view mirror. Yes. Take it off there, now plug it in to the USB slot right there on the dash. **WOW! A L.E.D screen with** *Yup Laser vision. Top of the line.* **Wow   Sweet tronics ... For a dragon fly...**

Ok ya see that chart. It shows my Past and current owners. I was owned by woman with three kids and a creepy husband. See the split on the chart right there. That is where Daddy came into the picture and took me away from them. You see right there where it ends, if I stayed with that woman, One of her kids was scheduled to forget the door open. And I was a runner back then, so I was supposed to escape, run out into traffic, and get killed by a car.! **OH MY GOODNESS! ... That's awful...**

That's when Daddy adopted me. That gave me a whole different life. It changed everything... from that point in time on. Woof... **That is amazing.** *I can show you how your life could have been Jayden...* **Thanks Edgar! But, I would rather not know! Besides my life with Mommy and Daddy was the best it could ever be, and IF YOU THINK My Mommy & Daddy were not nice, well**....*Woo, Woo.... WOOF! ...... Jayden! Jayden! Don't get all crazy on me! They were my Mommy and Daddy also....* **WOOF.... Okay Sorry. Sorry Edgar, I was having flash backs of the Pen and my first mean humans.**

OH...O.K. Hold on tight! We are entering the Earth's atmosphere. Bang ... boom.... **We are here already? I**

thought you said it was a long trip....... *But it was.... That was 2 months on earth...You see...Things slow down for us, but speed up for our human on earth. That way, we are alive for as long as they live on earth. We get to watch over them, be their guardian angels until they come and join us. Whenever that time may be...Come on...Lets go find Daddy!*

Look. There's the house! And there's Daddy! Sitting in the back yard. Hold on Jayden! I'm going to swoop down and land next to him. Look. Look. There he is. **Hey Daddy! Hey Daddy! Look! Look! It's me Jayden. I am in the Dragonfly! I'm in here with Edgar!** *Jayden. JAYDEN! Stop yelling! He can't hear you.* **He can't?** NO. *He can't. Sorry.* **Fly over there, to his right, Get closer**. *Jayden. I'm telling you. It's not going to matter. He can't see us. He just sees a dragon fly. But he can....* **Edgar look! He is looking right at us. Daddy! Daddy! It's me Jayden. I'm in the dragon fly with Edgar.... WAIT!**

Why is he crying? This is so sad! .... I can't watch this! It hurts too much! Besides, you said it has been 2 months! Why is he still crying? You said it has been 2 months! He can't still be crying over me! I'm just a dog... *Oh but Jayden. You were more than just a dog to them. You were his best buddy, his best friend, he lived and breathed to care for your every need. He loved you more life itself! You were like a child to both of them...*

Hey! Who is that coming in the yard? *Oh, that is one of Daddy's best friend, Lee.* **Yah... I know Lee!** *He has come over to comfort him; just as he did when I passed away.... he still looks the same. He got a little older looking and lost a little hair, but other than that he still looks good.* **Look... EDGAR. He is looking right at us. They are both just staring. And now they are laughing at us! Do you think they know it's us in here**? *Maybe. But I doubt it! Humans think dragonflies are magical or something. That's why I picked the dragonfly. You see, we could have come back as anything we wanted to....* **Hey look. They are taking our picture. And they are laughing again...** *Wow.*

Maybe they do know it is us in here! … **Yes, I think he does. Can he hear us**? *No…Well I don't think he can.*

So what do we do now? *You just say what you want to say and feel what you want him to feel. Just like when you were on earth. They love you, so they still have that connection to your thoughts and your feelings.* **I am all choked up Edgar... I don't know what to say now. Can we just sit here for a while?** *Sure thing girl. This is your day….*

Daddy looks so sad. I don't want to make him cry anymore. *It is not Daddy you need to worry about! It's Mommy! She took it really hard. When she was my Mommy, she didn't know how to make that connection. Don't get me wrong! She loved me very much. But it wasn't until she rescued you from the pen, that she felt the love that you had to offer. You filled her heart with love and kindness that only a mother can feel! And now that you're gone, she feels like she can never share that special feeling with* *another dog, ever again. She says" No other dogs can compare to my... (Jay Dee Jay)" So you have to let her know that every dog has the ability to communicate with humans. This is why we take the journey. To save the human heart ... To give hope.... To let them know, that inside every dog, there is never ending love, just waiting to be given.....*

So what do we do now? *Well it's almost supper time, Mommy should be getting home soon. So we wait until she gets here, then we go to work on her. I know that Daddy wants to adopt another dog from the pen. He hates seeing them locked up in cages. He can't even make eye contact with them, for fear of falling in love with ALL of them, I think Daddy would have a thousand dogs if he could,* **Yes, I think you are right Edgar! Woof. I just heard a car door**. *Yup... That's her, .WOOF... She hasn't changed in almost 20 years!* **How do you think I stayed so sexy all these years? We used to run almost every day!** *You do look good Miss Jayden!* **Some days I would have to drag her around the block! But she was easy, I would just give her my sad, puppy dog face when she wanted to cut our walks short...** *Ok I am gonna fly in closer. Just* *think positive thoughts and she will feel them .Just like when we were on the other side.*

MOMMY! It's me JAYDEN! I am in here! In the dragonfly, with Edgar! I LOVE YOU! *Jayden STOP yelling! She can't hear you. She can only feel your thoughts. Just like before.* **Really! Because I could have sworn she looked right at me.** *COME ON Jayden! A talking dragonfly, Nobody would believe her ...especially Daddy....* **I don't know! He was talking to us earlier.** *Yah, but he had been drinking with Lee. Do you remember New Year's Eve? Do I have to say anymore? OK, now let's try this again.* **Ok here it goes. Can I think out loud!** *OK Jayden, if that works for you, Talk out loud...* **Ok...Thanx Edgar.**

MOMMY, MOMMY! It's JAYDEN! *I said talk! Not scream...* **Ok Sorry! This is Jayden, Mommy I want you to know, I made it over the rainbow OK. I know how much you loved me, and would never betray me. But you need to get another rescue dog .You need to make Daddy happy! He**

needs a dog in his life. He needs someone to keep him company in the truck. A dog to love him and be man's best friend, I promise you Mommy. When you find the right dog, you will know! You will connect from the second you meet. Just like when I was in the Pen. Remember! I sat down for you and you shook my paw. I gave you my cutest smile and I knew I had you, right there & then... So when Daddy takes you looking, (and he will) Remember this. Dogs are just like people. We each have our own personalities and quirks. So look deep into their eyes and read their body language. If they are wagging, their tails and they have a big smile on their face. They Love you, it's that simple... So don't let all that love waste away in a cage. When all they want to do...Is share it with you ...

OK Edgar... Do you think I got thru to her? *Let's hope so. Only time will tell. OK Jayden, We have to head back over the bridge. Say your good byes. But just remember! They will always be able to feel you in their hearts and thoughts. So you will always be there for them.* **But I don't want to go...Mommy & Daddy are still so sad, and it's**

all my fault. *Trust me Jayden, the sooner we head back the sooner they will start the healing process. When Daddy put me down, he felt so bad, he waited a whole year before he rescued you. I had to coax him along...*

Wait Edgar! What does that mean (Put me down)? I heard the doctor say that to Daddy and he got all mad and (picked me up) off the doctors table and we left the office really fast...

Ha...Jayden, You are so cute. When a human puts you down they are helping us over the rainbow bridge. **You mean they are KILLING US?** *Well in a good way...YES...* **WOOF... I knew I should have bitten that mean ole witch doctor right in the butt when I had the chance! I couldn't figure out why Mommy & Daddy were so sad.** *Yes Jayden. They do feel bad when they have to make that decision. But when we are old and sick, it is the right thing to do. You see, before we relied on humans for food & shelter. We live out in the wild, and we had to*

KILL for our food, if you were not Strong enough to kill for food, YOU were the food... **EDGAR! That's terrible!** *Sorry Jayden. But that's the way it was hundreds of years ago. With the help of humans, we live so much longer. How long do you think you would have survived on the streets? Eating out of trash cans and sleeping under cars!*

WOOF! How do you know about that Edgar? I never told you about my days on the streets... *Ha-ha I looked at your dog tags. You lived a pretty nice life there on earth Jayden. Heck, you're almost 17 yrs. old.* **Yah Life was pretty sweet living with Mommy & Daddy.** *It sure was Jayden. I lived to be almost 16. You see the doctor wanted to put me down when I was about 14. But Daddy talked him into giving me shot's and Physical therapy. I had to take it easy and not walk on my leg at all. Daddy would carry me in and out of the house, every day for months. Heck! At one time, Daddy had duct tape holding my leg to my body so it wouldn't hurt me. Ha...* **Woof... yeah that's funny, Daddy is a fighter! He doesn't like to let go. And he especially does not like to lose the fight...**

Speaking of letting go; we have to go back over the rainbow. And it is a long trip back. We have lots of work ahead of us so let's go. Yell your goodbyes, Even though they can't hear you. **Good-bye Mommy. Good-bye Daddy. I love you.** *I love you too Mom and Dad...* **Hey Edgar...You said they cannot hear us.** *Yes. I know. It just feels so good. Being back here, in my old backyard, seeing them both still together.* **OK Edgar, let's go before YOU start blubbering.** *Okay Jayden. Warp speed to the Rainbow Bridge. We have to find a rescue dog to fix Mommy and Daddy...*

Wow, that was fast. For a dragonfly! Does this thing have a hemi or what?... *No silly, it runs on the dreams and aspirations of its occupants.* **What does that mean?** *Oh never mind. You will learn that later on. But for right now we have to find a rescue dog for Mommy and Daddy. Woof. Come on in here.*

Woof! Nice computer set up... What is that? *That my friend is a 275 GHz Mac Book Pro with 25 K Retina display... linked to a 40 inch led touch screen* *with thought processing, Laser vision, Wi-Fi and hologram capabilities....* **Woof...that's amazing. I've never even heard of anything like that ....***Nobody on earth has ever heard of these yet either. We get all latest and greatest gadgets from the dream team, before you get any of them on earth.* **How can that be Edgar?** *I'm sure you have heard of Albert Einstein? Nikolai Tesla? Steven Jobs? ...***Yes... They were some of the smartest guys in the world.**

Well...They have a cloud right down the street. They make all these crazy gadgets and inventions and let us try them out first. But, usually some crazy medium leaks out the information down to earth. Next thing you know HP or Macintosh, comes out with it, says it's their idea... But it's not! It all comes from up here.... **Wow! That is amazing Edgar, I think I'm going to like my job...**

Ok... Hit that green button over there that will pull down the main menu. Now I am going to punch it up on the hologram. **Wow that is so cool... It's as if he is sitting right in front of us.** *Yah, Space age cool, Huh...This is years ahead of human technology. OK, you see this dog. He is in the Pen in Providence.* **Woof. Hi, buddy.** *He can't hear you*

Jayden. He is a digital reproduction of the rescue dog in Providence. It's being broadcast in actual time, so we see and actually feel His Spirit. You know! So we can check him out. Look into his eyes, make the connection. Make sure he is just right for Mommy and Daddy. **Wow you are so smart Edgar.** *Don't worry Jayden, you will be learning all of this. Every day is a learning adventure up here...*

Ok Jayden, Mommy and Daddy are going to the Animal Shelter fundraiser this weekend and not all dogs are entered in the system. So load up the Dragonfly, we are going on a mission. I know Mommy is going, just to spend money to help the Animal Shelter, but I got the feeling Daddy is going dog shopping. So we had better go keep an eye on them. **Okay Edgar, I'm ready! Let's go!**

Woof. This is quite the turn out! Are all these people here to adopt a dog or a cat? *Sadly NO, Jayden. Most are here to support the Pen. They call it an animal shelter. But it's still a penitentiary if* *your dog...* **I hear that. Did you ever spend time in the Pen Edgar?** *No Jayden I was lucky.*

Daddy adopted me before I was scheduled to get hit by the car. He got me from a friend of a friend. So the only time I spent in a cage, was when I escaped and got caught by the dog officer. Daddy came and got me out right away. But believe me... I was scared! Because back then. If nobody came for you, you got in the Express line for the Rainbow Bridge. You know what I'm saying? **Let's not talk about those days Edgar...How could you kill a dog for NOT having humans at that moment in their lives? That's just not right. I'm glad people are changing their ways...**

OK... Now, let's find Mommy and Daddy... This is going to be hard with all these people here... **No it's not Edgar, just go by the jewelry section. You're bound to find Mommy at one of the vendors, spending money!** *.... Hey girl... I like the way you think. You're catching on fast! Hey look. There she is.* **But where is Daddy? I don't see him. Woof... Look. There he is. He is picking up a little**

**beagle puppy, that is the way it was in the pen.
All the cute little puppies get chosen first.**

*This is where you come in Jayden. Think of what
you want for Daddy. And he will feel your thoughts.*
Okay, Daddy, Daddy, *(here she goes with that
yelling again)... Jayden! He can't...! ...Oh never mind!
Keep yelling!* **Daddy put down that puppy! You
DON'T want him. He is going to poop all over
your house and chew up all of your things**. .
*Jayden! Jayden! What are you doing? You're supposed
to help Daddy get a new dog. Not talk him out of it!*
**You just keep flying this crazy dragonfly. I know
what I'm doing....** *BUT...* **Daddy! You are not a
beagle person...Do not get a puppy...Don't do it....**

*Look Jayden! You made him put the puppy
down. And now Mommy is making him leave. Now
what Jayden? We had them right where we wanted
them.* **You just trust me Edgar. I know how things
work at the Pen. That puppy is only been in here
for maybe a week. Before you know it, He will**

have a nice home, while the smarter, well behaved, older dog will be sitting in that cage for months and months. Do you know what that's like? It's horrible, it's scary and it's very lonely... *I'm sorry Jayden. You do have life experience in the Pen. I guess I wasn't looking at it from that side of the cage, so to speak.*

OK. What now? *We have to go back to the drawing board. Let's plan this next trip a little better. Now that we are on the same page. Ok Jayden*? **Ok Edgar ... I'm sorry I barked at you. I am just doing what is in my heart, for the good of the rescue dog and the good of Mommy and Daddy.** *No, you did the right thing Jayden. I guess it's just...I wanted them to be happy again. I wasn't thinking of the rescue dog. Thanks Jayden. For teaching this old dog new tricks.* **No problem Edgar. Just get this crazy dragonfly back over the rainbow so we can make a new plan, also because I am getting hungry!** *Yes my Lady... Your royal graciousness... Full speed ahead.* **Don't be a smart aleck ...THAT'S my job!** *WOOF Yes your majesty. This is a SWEET DEAL... I'm really liking this angel stuff.*

Woof... Hey Edgar! I think I got the hang of this fancy computer stuff, I invited Jobbsy and Einstein over for coffee the other day. They showed me a few tricks. *That was nice of them. They are pretty cool dudes, huh...* **Steve is pretty down to earth. But that Einstein is one strange dude. What's up with his hair? It looks like he got too close to one of Tesla's electrical experiments. Well, anyways, so here is what I found out.**

Mommy and Daddy are going to Providence Animal shelter to find a dog. I hacked into Mommy's Phone calendar and message box, Daddy's too. *Wow Jayden, You're a pretty good operator already.* **Thanks Edgar...**

So Saturday morning, they are going to the Providence pen. And Daddy has a message in his voice mail box. It says, a friend of a friend, has a dog going to the pen if she can't find a good home for her. It has a name and address, but no

information on the dog. And I checked, she is not in the system yet. *So we have to go watch over them.* YES...So I will go get the Dragonfly warmed up. *Woof...Jayden... Who said you could drive?* Oh I forgot to tell you. The Dream Team taught me how to drive the Dragonfly. Boy that Tesla has one cool car collection, Huh... I promised him I would bring him back some Cuban cigars for teaching me how to drive this thing... *Not a chance Missy, We are NOT going to Cuba, let's get going.*

Hey Jayden, easy on the clutch. Sorry Edgar, Did I spill your Perrier water? Oopsie...My bad. This thing is touchy when it get windy out. WOOF...You just keep an eye out for them. Her calendar app said 11 am. They should be here any minute...Woof...That's them over there. They just pulled in. I'm going to swing around over there next to the cages. They should be coming thru the door any second.

There they are. Awww... Look at Daddy's face. He still looks so sad! *I think he is sad for the dogs in the cages. Oh my God, look at how small these cages are! Did you have to stay in a small cage like that Jayden?* **Yes I did. For quite a long time too. Well at least they're clean. And they are warm and out of the elements. Hey... Where are they going? They're leaving already. Daddy couldn't even look them in the eyes.** *I wonder why they didn't even look around? There are some cute dogs in there. And their next appointment isn't till 12:30.*

I think I know why Edgar, because every dog in there was a Pit-bull. *What's wrong with Pit Bulls? Daddy had a 3 pit bulls growing up as a kid.* **I know he did. But certain towns will not let you have pit bulls, and your insurance company will drop you if they find out you have one.** *Are you kidding me? When did all this happen?* **This Pittie from the Pen told me, that rich people used to fight them against each other for their sick entertainment. And some drug dealers would get them and make them really mean. So they could protect their drugs from thieves.**

Now they have a bad reputation for themselves. *But it's not their fault, they were just doing what their humans told them to do.* **I know! I know, but it's hard to change people's minds. They hear about one mean pit-bull and think they are all mean. I know, that's not fair, because I know some pretty mean Yorkie's. And they bite people all the time. Okay, so what do we do now?** *Let's just go to the next appointment and wait for Mommy and Daddy to get there. Maybe we can poke around a little bit and check out this dog.* **Okay let's go....**

LOOK! Is that it? **NO, there it is. It says number 2173 Old Pine road on Mommy's calendar app, so this must be the place.** *OH great, it's on the second floor. Hey, buzz around back, maybe we can see in the windows. Look out for that branch!* **Hey I'm still not used to this clutch. The pedals are sticking too. What did they do? Sub this dragonfly job out to Henry Ford?** *You woman drivers are all alike. Not so fast. If you crash this thing we are in big trouble...*

Ok, pull up...EASY! Now land on that window sill over there... WOOF   Ohhh Man... Can you smell that? **Yeah I can smell it, Right thru the closed window, can you imagine how bad it smells inside? Look over there. That's a cage in the corner. It looks like that thing hasn't been cleaned for weeks. Yuck. They just keep putting newspaper down to soak up everything. That's horrible. I think I'm going to be sick. EDGAR! We have to get that dog out of this house. Even the pen would be a better place than this.**

Quick, fly around the other side. We'll see if we can spot her thru the other window. Wait! Mommy and Daddy just pulled up. They're early! **Hold on...This piece of space junk is acting up...** *Get down there! Closer to Daddy.* **I'm trying! I'm trying!** *You have to tell him, they need to get this dog out of there...* **I KNOW... I KNOW...I think the clutch is slipping...** *Jayden you have to get closer. He won't be able to sense you from this far away. WOOF....* **All**

right...I got it...Don't get your panties in a bunch...

Look out for that electrical wire. Pay attention Jayden... Lookout for that branch! You're driving crazy! Don't crash this thing! I don't know what would happen if we couldn't get back over the rainbow! **I got it. I got it. Keep it in your Biscuit bag. Can't you see it's windy out today?** *Get down there closer... No, No ...Even closer. Quick Jayden, yell to Daddy, before he closes the door.... Woof... Too late. Now what?* **HOLD ON! I'll swing around back.**

We have to get through to him! Where is he? They're not in this room! *Hurry... Go over to the other window.* **Look! They're way over the other side... Woof... and there's the dog! Awww, what a cutie she is. And she looks so friendly. Awww... Look how she's smiling at Mommy and Daddy. The poor little thing, she just wants to get out of there so bad. She's trying to connect to Daddy but he's busy talking to the owner. Mommy's just looking around at all the filth.** *Quick Jayden! Do that yelling thing you do! Maybe we can get thru to them from here.* **Daddy!   Daddy. You have to get this**

dog out of here! Edgar. I don't think we have a connection. He is too far away. *Move up to the middle of the window. Yah right here. Try it now...*Daddy...DADDY. Its ME! Jayden. You need to get this poor dog out of this place. Help her! Please! DADDY... *I do not think it's working...* We are not close enough. We need to get Daddy to move closer to the window, so I can connect with him. *How can we do that?* I don't know Edgar, but I can't let them leave here. NOT without that dog! *But Jayden, he can't hear you!* Well he can't hear me. But I know MY Daddy. And MY Daddy can see ME!

Jayden! What are you going to do? Hold on to your Perrier water, Edgar! We are about to see if Einstein put airbags in this contraption. *What are you gonna do Jayden?* You may want to buckle your seatbelt Edgar. Because we are about to sign adoption papers!

Bbbbzbzbzzzzz... Bang!   Daddy look! Look over here....*Jayden! What are you? A lunatic or something...* Bbzzzzz... Bang.. Crash... DADDY! *Jayden stop! You're going to kill us.* I don't care Edgar! And besides that... I am ALREADY dead! ...bbbzzzzz. ...bang... DADDY! Look over here! ..... It's me Jayden. *STOP! STOP ...This is CRAZY...He doesn't know its US in here, JAYDEN....*HOLD ON Edgar.

Bbbbzzzz... Bang, crash. DADDY! *JAYDEN! STOP smashing into the window! You're gonna break the dragonfly...DOG GONE IT! Jayden! If you crash this thing, we've got NO WAY TO GET BACK!* Hold on Edgar. I'm going to circle around... Full steam ahead. *OH MY GOD! YOU'RE CRAZY!* Bbzzzz... HOLD ON EDGAR...BBzzzz BANG! Boom! Crash!...

DADDY.... Daddy it's ME! Jayden! I'm with Edgar in the dragonfly. Remember you saw us in the backyard. *Jayden look! He's coming closer to the window. KEEP Yelling!* Daddy! Daddy! Oh please Daddy! Save this poor little dog. She is stuck in this apartment all day long in that tiny smelly cage. She just wants somebody to LOVE...

Look Jayden, Daddy is walking right up to the window. WOOF! Now He is pointing at us. He's calling Mommy over to the window, and now he is saying something. Jayden quick! Talk to them... Tell them how bad she has it here... **Mommy! Daddy! Please, Please! Rescue this dog. She can have my old bed and all my chew toys... but please! Just care for her as you did for me. Give her a place to call her own, give her lots of love, because I can tell she loves you. Please Daddy! Please. Edgar! Look! They are all staring right at us and laughing. Do you think they know it's us in here?** *You know what Jayden...I think they do ...I think you got thru to them...This is amazing...***Mommy is smiling and giving Daddy big kisses. I don't believe it. LOOK! I think they are going to take her. They are! Mommy and Daddy are rescuing the dog! Daddy is taking her leash and they are walking out the door! Yeahaaa !!!**

WOOF! I cannot believe this! We did it! Yahoo... WE did it Edgar! We got them to SAVE the DOG! .... *NO Jayden ...YOU did it! That was DOG CRAP CRAZY! But you did it!* **HEY! What can I say? I'm like my Daddy! I don't like to lose!** *Speaking of losing. I think we lost power on that last crash to the window.* **Well what NOW? We can't even follow Daddy home, to check on the new rescue dog...**

Woof... look...There she goes....Off with her new family **... Awww   That's where I used to sit, in the middle seat. Right in between the two of them ...GOOD BYE Mommy ...Good Bye Daddy...Take good care of her. I know she will love you with all her heart. You saved her from a life in the Pen...A life of abuse and neglect and for that, I will set your hearts free. Free to love another dog ...Freee too, free toooo... Sniff. I think I am going to cry Edgar. Sniff, sniff, I just gave away my Mommy and Daddy to another dog! Sniff, sniff ...** *NO YOU DIDN'T.* **I didn't?**

NO...Remember you will live in their hearts forever, you will always be a part of their lives and them a part of yours...And now you have a little sister to watch over...

I WHAT? *I said you have a* **... I HEARD WHAT YOU SAID...OH MY GOD I don't believe it! I have a SISTER...I can't believe it. I have a sister! WOOF... This is one of the greatest days of my life! I've got you for my Big Brother and Now I have a little sister... Yaahhhoooo...** *Hey! Save the celebrating for later. We have a big problem! We have to figure out how to get back over the rainbow!*

Oh, No problem Edgar, Jobbsie gave me a new gadget he made. I forgot what he called it, but if I just press this green button on my watch, and talk into your wrist. It sends him a Voice mail, a text message, a Tweet, an Instagram pic, a Face Book instant message, a Google earth map, a Digital... *OK...OK... enough techno babble, just press the button and Get us off this 2nd floor window sill!*

Before that bird over there see's us and thinks we are his afternoon snack ...Remember? We still look like a dragon fly to everybody else.

Even if that gadget doesn't work, I'm sure Einstein will come looking for us. I told him I was gonna let you drive the dragon fly. He is probably looking for us already. ha ha...You know how this dragonfly is his little baby. Just wait till he sees the damage! You could be in big trouble!

Sorry Edgar. I had to do it. For the dog, for Mommy and especially for Daddy! Did you see the big smile on his face as he was driving away? Now I can sleep at night, knowing Mommy and Daddy have a dog to help heal their broken hearts. To protect them. To Love them. *Yes Jayden. I did notice Daddy's big smile. It's a good feeling. Being a guardian angel!* **Yes it is Edgar ...Yes it is ...**

Hey guys, thanx for coming to the rescue... Sorry about crashing your dragon fly Mr. Einstein... But Hey,

Just think. You can build a better one! Get Jobsie to put all that fancy computer stuff in it, maybe some air bags! Hey Jobsie...Does this space age contraption have Wi-Fi and all that fancy computer software? Id likes to check up on my Little sister. *Hey, Jayden. What is her name anyway? In all the excitement, I forgot to check her records. Jayden, please push that green button next to the touch screen.* **Push this big button right here?** *Yes Jayden, thanks.*

HELLO...THIS IS CYRUS! HOW MAY I HELP YOU?

Wow! That is so cool... I knew a Cyrus in the Pen. Is that a hologram? It looks so real. *Yes, Just tell her what you want Jayden ...* **Ok, here it goes... Hi Cyrus, I want to check on my new Little sister...**

SORRY. HOLOGRAM DISPLAY IS NOT AVAILABLE FOR THAT APPLICATION... WOULD YOU LIKE TO LISTEN TO HER VOICE RECORDING? ... Yes Cyrus, Please ...*ONE MOMENT PLEASE... ...NOW LOADING ...*

Hi... My Name is Sheba. Yes that's right. I'm a dog... Your probably saying to yourself, Dogs can't talk never mind... write a book ... But if you are a true dog lover ......You know we can talk in our own little ways...

THE DOG WHISPERER

In her younger years. Jayden was a little hard to read because, she was so hyper and energetic. But as she got older, She got... or I should say we got, a little better at understanding her wants, needs and body language...The day I took her for a ride on the motorcycle, I really believe she was trying to talk to me ...She was a little freaked out at first. But then after a trip up and down the street...She put her head right on my shoulder and was Making these sounds from deep in her throat and whispered in my ear ...I have never heard that sound from ANY dog in my life...She was either saying

1. Let me drive this thing, 2. You're a CRAZY MAN....or 3. This is so Cool. I am having the best time of my LIFE. I believe it was ....This is SO COOL because, every time I started the motorcycle, she would get all happy and spin around in circles....I said to myself. OH NO! What have I done...I felt so bad not taking her for rides all the time. But it would take a long time to

remove the seat and strap the box down to the bike then remove it again.

Vacations and long weekends away from the house. Were always a challenge...From the shelter of the back porch she had access to the outside to do her thing. Well she would let me know she was mad by escaping from her 6 ft fenced in pen area and go sit on the front porch... (Kinda like...You can't hold me hostage while you're out having fun) So I put 2 feet of lattés on the top of that. So she climbed the fence and chewed a hole thru it and escaped. So I replaced the Latté's with wood making it 8 ft tall. She would still go over the top. So I put my big work ladders on top to make a cover. Then she would chew a hole in the fence to escape! Just to go sit on the front porch. OK Jayden... You WIN... You made your point...☺

This little poem is dedicated to Stewie

Run over the rainbow, and then you will see.

Samantha, Edgar and Jayden makes three...

Say Hi to them Stewie, Just from me...

You are forever in our hearts...

Run fast and Run free....

A special Thank You to Mikey Maguire for everything you have said and done to help me, inspire me, with this writing project. Also a special Thank you to all of my Facebook Friends...Your kind words keep me going.

This is a book of fiction and Fact's that only exist in the mind of the writer...All similarities to persons living or deceased are purely coincidental.

The Author: I John (Jay) Gafford am a born and raised in Attleborough . I grew up in a small family neighborhood and attended Attleboro High School. With Metal Fabrication being my major, English was never top on my list... I feel strange even saying, I AM WRITING A BOOK... During high school I may have written (maybe) 2 book reports. And they were probably plagiarized from the encyclopedia. (Yes, back then we didn't have the internet) Thanks to MS Words...spell check and templets...I am able to put out a half way decent manuscript .With the help of a lifelong friend we squeezed out most of the errors. I'm sure we missed quit a few...EAY nobody's perfect...

After years in the metal/welding trade, I started selling and rehabbing single and multifamily properties... Missing working with my hands, I bought a small welder and started making Recycled Metal Art. My art can be seen on my Face book page {Jays Garden Art –Custom metal Art work... In there you can see my version of the dragon fly, as I see it in the book...Made from a cars shock absorber spring, a few lawn mower blades, an Industrial handle of some sorts a few railroad spikes... Some nuts and bolts etc. etc.

Edgar and Jayden have told you most of my past...Before Edgar, My family had a beautiful American Pit Bull Terrier named Beauty...She only had one litter, but was left with the figure of a small cow....we kept two of her male Pups...One was aggressive towards other dogs, the Other could care less...we ended up selling the aggressor to a long distance trucker. The pup growled at the trucker when he walked in the door. He like that, cause he wanted a protective guard dog for his truck ...Beauty ended up crossing over from old age..

Multiple copies may be purchased with a discount for schools and book clubs by contacting the author directly on my Face Book page Thru a Dogs Eyes

Or by contacting Jay at Thruadogseyes@comcast.net

Published by BULL DOG Productions

72 Hope St Attleboro Mass 02703